THE BELONGING PROJECT

FINDING YOUR TRIBE AND LEARNING TO THRIVE

AMBERLY NEESE

Abingdon Women

Nashville

The Belonging Project
Finding Your Tribe and Learning to Thrive

ISBN 978-1-5018-9875-4

20 21 22 23 24 25 26 27 28 29 — 10 9 8 7 6 5 4 3 2 1
MANUFACTURED IN THE UNITED STATES OF AMERICA

Contents

About the Author

Amberly Neese is a speaker, humorist, and encourager with a passion for "GRINspiring" others. As a featured speaker for the Aspire Women's Events and the main host/comedienne for Marriage Date Night, two popular Christian events that tour nationally, she enjoys touching the hearts and minds and funny bones of people all over the country. The Bible says that laughter is good medicine, and she has found it's also like glue—helping the truths of God's Word to "stick." Amberly loves to remind women of the power and hope found in Scripture. Through a flair for storytelling and a love for Jesus, she candidly opens up her story alongside God's Word to encourage others in their walk with Him.

With a master's degree from Biola University, Amberly serves as an adjunct professor at Grand Canyon University and the chief experience officer at UCYC (United Christian Youth Camp). She and her husband, Scott, have two teenagers and live in Prescott, Arizona, where they enjoy the great outdoors, the Food Network, and all things Star Wars.

Follow Amberly:

 @amberlyneese

 @amberlyneese

 @Amberly Neese - Comedian and Speaker

Website   www.amberlyneese.com

Tour information can also be found at marriagedatenight.com and aspirewomensevents.com.

Introduction

Welcome to The Belonging Project!

Has the pursuit of the "perfect life" left you feeling depleted, disappointed, dissatisfied, and disconnected? Are you tired of being lonely and left out at work, home, church, and online? Are you hungry for true community, deeper connection with God, and friendships that are greater and more meaningful than just "likes" on social media? Are you ready for real connections with those around you? If so, then you're in the right place!

Let's be honest. Community is not always easy to find and maintain. We lead busy lives: soccer games, permission slips, work, hair appointments, garage sales, quiet time, grocery shopping, prayer, cooking, cleaning, orthodontist appointments, church events, time at the gym—they all add up to lives filled with activity and little margin for much else. So, how can we possibly have time or make time to include new people in our lives or to foster stronger friendships with those we already know? Well, the truth is, we have to prioritize it. I love social media, but at times it can be one of the greatest detriments to biblical community. Seeing posts from friends who had get-togethers where we were not invited can pierce our hearts and our pride. Such hurt can create bitterness and wane our desire to be with others.

Recently, I sent my mom a book on traveling with dogs. She and my stepdad just bought a beautiful RV and began traveling with their two cute dogs. The experience proved more than challenging to my mother, and she found herself frustrated and disappointed by a journey that was supposed to be fun. When I sent her the book, I just thought it would offer practical tips on how best to travel with canine companions, but it ended up including a wonderful reminder for my mother: "The difference between an ordeal and an adventure is attitude."[1] Wow. That is true, not just regarding dogs and RVs but also life and relationships. We have a choice every day to risk. To take an attitude of openness and choose community.

I began training for a one-day hike to the bottom of the Grand Canyon and back for my fiftieth birthday, and I needed to get as many miles on my feet and in my hiking boots as possible. One day, I was hiking on a hill near my home. As I approached the entrance to the trail, there were two ladies about twenty feet ahead of me. They were younger, thinner, and clearly more athletic.

I usually like to have a hiking buddy with me, but on this particular day, my hiking buddy was not feeling well, so I was on my own. However, I decided that the pace of these two women would be my goal for the day. If I could continue to maintain the twenty-foot margin between us, even if it meant no stopping, I knew that I would indeed have a great workout.

It was not easy. I usually stop two or three times up this particular hill, but because of these much stronger women, I kept pace. I was relieved and elated when we finally made it to the top of the hill. I was also winded. After catching my breath, I introduced myself to the ladies and thanked them for being such an inspiration to me. They looked at one another and laughed, admitting that they too had been challenged by the "mystery person" behind them; they had made a pact to stay ahead of me and continue their rapid pace so that I would not catch up with them. "You were our inspiration today," they said.

I see those ladies often as I trek the hiking trail closest to my home. Each time we smile, high-five, and spur one another on toward a faster pace. Community is designed to strengthen and inspire us.

Despite what we see in movies and magazines, where personal strength and winning are celebrated, we are created for community. We are meant to encourage one another, walk ahead of and behind one another, and create connections with one another. Yet even as part of a church, we often fall prey to societal patterns of comparison and competition and miss out on true community.

God has designed us for community. In fact, Jesus was so passionate about community that He not only chose disciples—twelve guys of varying backgrounds, personalities, and gifts, to walk with Him in His journey—He also instructed them to do likewise with others. He invited a myriad of others, including many women, to partner with Him in

ministry along His path. Through His teachings and the teachings of His followers, we have a blueprint for the community He has designed for us. This blueprint can be found in the phrases in the New Testament that include the words *one another*, such as love one another, encourage one another, serve one another, forgive one another, and many more.

The phrase "one another" is derived from the Greek word *allelon*, which means "one another...each other; mutual," or "reciprocally."[2] Appearing over one hundred times in the New Testament, this concept forms the basis of all true Christian community and has direct impact on our witness to the world. As we read in John 13:35, "By this everyone will know that you are my disciples, if you love one another."

In this study we will examine some of these "one anothers," grouping them into four themes:

- Find One Another
- Fellowship with One Another
- Forgive One Another
- Fortify One Another

Each week as we focus on one particular theme, we will explore relevant "one another" Scriptures and other related passages to help give us clarity on how we might live a life in community that is both fulfilling and fun. Together, we will dive into how to handle life when we feel dejected, disconnected, and dissatisfied so that we can find our tribe and learn to thrive.

Each day starts with a "One Another" verse, which sets the tone for the day, includes a Scripture focus and questions for reflection, and ends with a Call to Action. (The lessons are designed to be completed in about 20 minutes.) Then once a week you'll gather with your group to watch a video, discuss what you're learning, and pray together. The session outlines, which provide options for both a 60-minute and a 90-minute session, include discussion questions, activities, prayer prompts, and notes for the video segment. You'll find the outline for each session at the end of the personal lessons for that week.

If you're the facilitator or leader of your group, you'll want to check out the additional leader helps at the back of this book. Ideally group members should complete the first week of lessons before your first group session. This is because each video message complements the content that you have studied during the week. However, feel free to adapt the study as you wish to meet the needs of your particular group. The questions and activities will guide you in sharing your experiences and learnings together.

My own journey of examining the "one anothers" in the New Testament has been so rewarding. I have grown from studying God's Word and allowing Him to help me apply these verses to foster deeper, more meaningful connections with others. My prayer is that the same will be true for you. I am excited to embark on this Belonging Project with you!

Biblical Background

If we are to "find our tribe and learn to thrive," we need to go back to the beginning of Jesus's life and the vision He cast for His followers.

Throughout His time on earth, Jesus said things that seemed revolutionary (and downright crazy) to His contemporaries. He broke through cultural, political, and social barriers during His thirty years of life and three years of public ministry. His followers (including the apostle Paul, who penned many of the letters in the New Testament) followed suit. Their behaviors, practices, and words often flew in the face of the culture and helped shape history.

For one to completely grasp the departure that Jesus's words served in the culture of His day, we must first take a deeper look into the religious, social, and political climate from which Jesus came.

Jesus was born into a Jewish family in a small village, with two metropolitan cities a short distance from his home. Nazareth predominantly comprised people from the Jewish faith. When he was born, Judaism was a menagerie of various and often opposing social, political, and religious ideologies. At the time, there were four distinct factions of the Jewish faith: the Zealots, the Sadducees, the Pharisees, and the Essenes.

The Zealots were those involved in a movement that was much more revolutionary in nature. Violence, including armed rebellion, was the tool they would use to attempt to save Israel from the oppression of the Roman government. Today, we are aware of extremist groups in varying religious sects; the Zealots were one of those in Jesus's day.

The Sadducees were also part of the climate in the time of Jesus. They were guided more by practicality than ideals; many scholars deem them the least religious group, characterized by their lack of faith in resurrection. One of my college professors used the name of the group and a wordplay to help us remember them by saying: "the Sadducees do not believe in life after death, which makes them *sad, you see?*" They were often wealthy religious leaders and aristocrats who sought to maintain their standings, possessions, and influence through compromise with Rome. Most of the members of the Sanhedrin were from the Sadducee group. However, they were powerful leaders in that society, so it is possible that they viewed Jesus as a threat to their status and power. They spent much more time concentrated on the affairs of the day and how they were viewed by others.

The Pharisees were the spiritual powerhouses of the day. Most of the Scribes—the men chosen specifically to copy the Scriptures, an amazing honor at this time in history—were Pharisees. The Pharisees sought to live a life of obedience to the Holy Scriptures (Jewish law). They disagreed with the Zealots in that they did not believe in violence as a means to peace; and they opposed the Sadducees because of their religious compromise. Their painstaking emphasis on obedience to the Law had the potential to create highly spiritual people, indeed; but it also could create a legalistic approach that placed law over love.

Finally, there were the Essenes, who avoided the violence of the Zealots, the power-hunger of the Sadducees, and the legalism of the Pharisees by placing themselves in a monastic-like setting. They removed themselves completely from Jewish society and practiced their faith apart from society as a whole. John the Baptist, Jesus's cousin, was an Essene.

This is the religious climate into which Jesus was born.

The political climate was also in tumult.

The Romans at this time were organized into a two-tiered system of government to exercise power and control. The two tiers consisted of both Roman overseers and Jewish leaders. The family of Herod the Great grew to prominence in this season, a season filled with brutality, injustice, immoral behavior, and religious oppression. One of Herod's family members, Pontius Pilate, played a leading role in the crucifixion of Jesus. Another of the sons in this clan, Herod Antipas, was responsible for the beheading of John the Baptist.

This season bred heaviness in the hearts of all Jewish people; it created disunity and fear. For the Romans, any new leader would serve as a threat to the existing leadership; each new Roman king brought bloodshed and tyranny. It is on this canvas that the background of Jesus's ministry is painted.

With this perspective of Jesus's day, it is easy to see why the Jewish leaders were so quick to be threatened by Him. They were concerned that with new teachings would come violence and judgment from Rome. They also were afraid of groups of people banding together to instigate coups.

According to some scholars, those in authority—both civic and religious leaders—had complete justification for concern. The tumult in Jerusalem included unrest and violence both foreign and domestic. Massacres by rivals in the first century alone took thousands of lives. The presence of Jesus undoubtedly made those already nervous even more worried about the ramifications of a "revolutionary" like Jesus.

It is because of this cultural climate that the words of Jesus were so revolutionary.

In a time of unrest, dissension, fear, and uncertainty, the "one anothers" in the New Testament stand in contrast to the political, social, and religious timbre in Rome at this time. While leaders were afraid of groups banding together, Jesus and His followers encouraged believers to live in community. His words still bring us hope in the tumult of the political, social, and religious unrest of today.

Jesus's words were also revolutionary when it came to another topic: women. At this time in history, a woman was considered property, and her testimony was not admissible in court, for it had no validity. (I am so thankful I was not born at that time, for I am a loud, opinionated woman, and I am afraid I would have gotten myself into a lot of trouble!)

As we embark on this study of relationships with other women, it's important for us to take note that Jesus valued women. He spoke to the woman at the well, healed the woman with a bleeding disorder, honored and instructed Mary and Martha, let a sinful woman wash his feet, saved an adulterous woman from certain death by stoning, and even appeared to women first after He was resurrected from the dead. We matter to Jesus, as do our relationships with one another. So let's commit to prioritize those relationships and seek to build authentic, God-honoring community!

Week 1

Find One Another

Friendship Through the
Lens of Biblical Community

Memory Verse

Be devoted to one another in love. Honor one another above yourselves.

(Romans 12:10)

Day 1: Finding Community

Today's "One Another"

Be devoted to one another in love. Honor one another above yourselves.

(Romans 12:10)

When my husband and I first moved back to Arizona, I loved my job, but I did not enjoy the pain of loneliness I experienced. We left a thriving friendship community in California, with a plethora of friends with whom we enjoyed doing life; I was really struggling to find such a community in our new town.

I felt like a junior high schooler at a dance. I was standing against the wall, wanting someone, anyone, to ask me to dance. (For the record, when I was a junior high schooler, I was a foot taller than the boys in my class, so I am very familiar with this scenario!)

I pleaded with God. I whined to God. I bargained with God. I asked Him for wisdom regarding where I should go to find a community of girlfriends. I even gave Him my list of "wishes." I wanted a group of committed followers of Christ who were strong, fun, and happened to have space in their group for someone like me.

Finally, I found Krista. She is smart, beautiful, and a truly terrific wife and mom. She is a lawyer, an active member of our community, and a woman with deep convictions for families and justice. And she is truly crazy about Jesus. I would go so far as to say that she is a "love, shove, and point above" kind of friend—a person who loves me enough to encourage me, call me on my junk (and love me enough not to allow me to stay in that junk), and consistently point me to Jesus.

She brought with her an amazing friend group. But I never felt like I was part of it. They had all been friends for years, had daughters in the same dance troupes and sons in the same classes, and frankly, made *way* more money than I did. They would let me come to their gatherings, but I always felt like a visitor.

That is, until the day that Krista had a really disappointing loss. She had applied for a position for which she was by far the strongest, most qualified candidate with the longest service record. And she didn't get the job. Needless to say, she was not only disappointed; she was mad. It was on this day, one of the hardest days of her life, that I found community.

Minutes after we received the news, another woman in the group, an equally fantastic human being and pursuer of Jesus, sent out a group text. It was simple and straightforward. It said, "Let's all meet at Krista's house at five." And we did. One by one, we all showed up with hugs, prayers, encouragement, and laughter. As you can well imagine, she was not interested in the laughter at first, but we just sat with her in her disappointment. In her anger. In her mourning. In her shouts of injustice. And we cried too. We reminded her how loved she is and how good God is. We let her rant. We each took turns encouraging her. We sat in silence and prayed.

I left that night feeling fuller, more encouraged, and finally part of something for which I had prayed for a long time.

Do you have a best friend or group of close friends? If so, how did you meet?

If not, have you ever had a best friend or group of close friends? How did you meet?

What are the attributes you look for in a friend?

What characteristics do you possess that make you a good friend?

On a scale of 1–10, how satisfied are you with your current friendships? Why?

I still tear up at the thought of that evening with my new friend group. It was a beautiful example of how the body of Christ is called to be devoted to one another and honor one another.

Read Romans 12:10 in the margin. What are some specific ways you have both shown and received devotion and honor in relationships?

Be devoted to one another in love. Honor one another above yourselves.
(Romans 12:10)

Shown   **Received**

If you struggled with any part of that exercise, you're not alone. We do not always see devotion and honor in the everyday of relationships. It is a struggle to fulfill Romans 12:10 when people disappoint us and loneliness plagues us. But you and I are not designed to live in isolation. In fact, we cannot fully live the Christian life in isolation. The "one anothers" in the New Testament clearly show that we are designed to work together as a Body, and we are most healthy when we function this way. Because it's not easy, there are some things we need to recognize. First, we need to recognize that God created us for community.

The story of Creation in the Book of Genesis illustrates community from the beginning. When God created man and woman, He made them in community to be companions in work, life, and procreation—the further building of community. They were in community with each other and with God.

And God is the master example of community. The very nature of who God is involves relationship: God the Father, Son, and Holy Spirit. The triune (or three-part) God is an eternal being in relationship. Isolation and loneliness are the opposites of God and the purposes He has for each of us.[1]

Once we recognize we were created for community, we need to get in touch with our need for it. It is often biblical community that allows us to grow, get feedback, follow examples, and look more like Jesus. Even beyond the church, living in community with others outside of the faith can shape us and mold us.

Although we need community, it requires vulnerability to put ourselves out there in search of it. Old wounds, hurt feelings, and insecurities all play a role in what makes it difficult. We all have been hurt by someone who spoke an unkind word, criticized us, or failed to include us in their plans. So although we can recognize we were made for community and need it, we also must face the fact that it can be risky to put yourself out there.

When my husband resigned as a pastor, for the first time in our married lives we had to find a church home. With our strong opinions, woundedness from the last church, and two kids in tow, trying to find a community was like speed dating for Jesus each Sunday morning. We would try on each building, children's ministry program, and worship service for a fit. Ugh. It was worse than bathing suit shopping. Well, not really. *Nothing* is worse than bathing suit shopping, but it was bad.

But we were hungry for community.

Abram in the Old Testament knew the importance of having others in his life. He surely recognized he was made for community and needed it; but until God called him to a new land, he may not have recognized the risk involved.

In Genesis 12:1-4, we find a seventy-five-year-old Abram who was asked by God to take a big risk and find new community.

Read Genesis 12:1-4. What did God ask Abram to give up?

If you were Abram, which part of this call from God would be the most daunting? Why?

What were the blessings God promised to give Abram in exchange for his willingness to step out in faith?

God asked Abram to leave everything and almost everyone he knew, the safety of his community, and the "known" for an unknown land. How scary! Fortunately for Abram and for us, his story shows that although it might seem risky, there is always a reward in obedience when God calls us to do something bold.

The Book of Genesis is filled with the promises God gave Abram. In Genesis 12:7, a few verses later, God promises to give the land to Abram's descendants. Again, he and his wife are without children—and eligible for AARP at this point! In Genesis 13:2 and 14-17, God promises to bless Abram. In Genesis 15:4-6 and 18, God promises that Abram and Sarai's descendants will be as numerous as the stars. In Genesis 17:1-8 and 15-16, God gives the childless couple new names and affirms the promises He has made to them, this time using particles of dust to explain how numerous their descendants will be. In Genesis 21, we see the birth of their son, Isaac. Despite the fact that Sarah is "past the age" for having children, God allowed her to conceive and carry a son.

Throughout their interactions, God often reminded Abraham of His power and abilities and called Abraham to trust Him—even as he left one community for another. Without exception, there was a long waiting period between promise and fulfillment. Abraham and Sarah could have given up but instead, their faith was strengthened. God blessed their vulnerability and trust.

For most of us, community is hard to find wherever we may live. It takes confidence and a willingness to be vulnerable to others. As Paul reminds us in Romans 12:10, "Be devoted to one another in love. Honor one another above yourselves." Devotion in love takes a desire to foster friendship, be vulnerable, and listen to God. Honoring others above ourselves may mean putting our insecurities aside and focusing on the call of God to connect with others. And it's a call meant to bless each and every one of us.

Call to Action

- Ask God to show you how you can add to your community of friends.
- Call or connect with at least one person in your church and ask how you can pray for him or her. Pray with him or her on the phone or in person.
- Make a list of people who might be good additions to your community of friends. Include people from your church, work-place, and neighborhood or area. Pray for each of them—not only that they might become your friend but also that God would bless them.

Scripture Focus

Acts 2

Day 2: No Judgment

Today's "One Another"

Therefore let us stop passing judgment on one another. Instead, make up your mind not to put any stumbling block or obstacle in the way of a brother or sister.

(Romans 14:13)

There is a chain of convenience stores I am obsessed with—like totally "cuckoo for Cocoa Puffs" over. I know, of all things to be crazy about, to pick a convenience store! But this one is exceptional. It has the largest selection of beverages I've ever seen in all of my life and a giant frozen cappuccino for less than two bucks. It could not be any

better, unless there was one located closer to my home; the nearest one is about fifty miles away.

I am sure if there was a twelve-step program for those with a convenience store addiction, I would lead the meetings.

But not for all convenience stores, just this specific chain. I love their friendly attitude, I love the way they make eye contact with everyone who walks in, I love the cleanliness of their bathrooms, and again, I cannot get enough of those frozen cappuccinos; it is like the land of milk and honey for me. Delicious.

It was on one of my trips into this beverage mecca when I saw her. From the front, she was an attractive woman with a nice smile and a cute outfit. However, when she turned toward the clerk to pay for her purchase, I noticed that the bottom of the skirt she was wearing was tucked into the waistband. When I say I could see everything underneath that skirt, I am not exaggerating. The color of her underwear, the misalignment of the pantyhose hem in the back, the extra pounds she was carrying—all of it was visible.

Everyone in the busy convenience store with the exception of the clerk and her saw what I saw. And no one said anything. No one felt compelled to let her know that she was about to enter the parking lot with her dignity tucked into the back of her skirt.

I'm usually the type of friend who lets you know when there's broccoli in your teeth, but there was something about the fact that this woman was a stranger to me that silenced me. For the first time in my adult life, I was speechless. Completely unable to utter a word.

I shot a glance toward my coworker who was with me and mouthed, "Should we say something?" She shrugged. But I knew I needed to tell the woman about her wardrobe malfunction. I knew that although I would never see her again and I had seen more of her than I ever wanted to, she needed to know. So I followed her to her car. I am confident that I looked like a complete weirdo or stalker, but I didn't care. The Golden Rule kept repeating itself in my brain, and I knew that if I, indeed, were displaying my backside to the general public, I would want someone to tell *me*.

So I did it. I kindly told her that the hem of her skirt was tucked into the waistband and she might want to pull it down. As she reached back and felt the skirt wadded up, her eyes widened. The color completely drained from her beautiful face. And then it rushed back. Just in her cheeks. She spoke softly, "Do you think anybody noticed?" I paused before I responded, thinking to myself, *Do I tell her that everybody in the greater metropolitan area noticed? Do I tell her that I need to see a therapist for the things I saw?*

Rather than passing judgment and offering words that might embarrass, I simply replied, "I am not certain, but I do know that I noticed, and I know I would want you to tell me if the roles were reversed."

The grateful words that followed seemed to come from a deep part of her heart. Though it had not been easy for me to say, her gratitude more than made up for my discomfort.

By the way, if my skirt is ever tucked into my waistband, you better believe I want you to tell me!

Therefore let us stop passing judgment on one another. Instead, make up your mind not to put any stumbling block or obstacle in the way of a brother or sister.
(Romans 14:13)

Read Romans 14:13 in the margin and answer the following questions:

Have you ever felt "judged" by a friend or colleague? If so, how did it make you feel?

When was the last time you had to point out something uncomfortable to someone? Was she or he appreciative?

Why do you think it is hard for us to tell people things that are embarrassing?

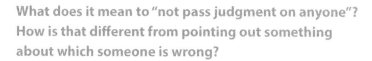

What does it mean to "not pass judgment on anyone"? How is that different from pointing out something about which someone is wrong?

In the Sermon on the Mount in Matthew 5, Jesus instructs us to avoid judging others in a manner or to a standard that we would not want applied to ourselves. One commentary sheds some light on how and why we should view our responsibilities to our fellow believer when it comes to judgment: "When we admonish or rebuke, we do it over *clear Scriptural principles*, not over *doubtful things*. We may offer *advice* to others about doubtful things, but should never judge them."[2]

This does not mean we should not pour wisdom into those in our community who are acting in a manner inconsistent with the teachings of Jesus.

Read 2 Timothy 4:2 and Romans 15:14 in the margin. What did the apostle Paul encourage us to do, and how are we to do it?

Preach the word; be prepared in season and out of season; correct, rebuke and encourage—with great patience and careful instruction.
    (2 Timothy 4:2)

So, what does this "instruction" look like, practically? How do we avoid destroying the community we are attempting to build?

The Book of Acts is the narrative of the early church. It serves as such a beautiful blueprint of healthy, mutually beneficial community, and it gives us perspective on how to strike this balance.

Read Acts 2:42-47. What is your response to the description of this community of early believers?

I myself am convinced, my brothers and sisters, that you yourselves are full of goodness, filled with knowledge and competent to instruct one another.
    (Romans 15:14)

Honestly, when I read the account of the first church sharing every-thing, I vacillate between being inspired by the idea that they "shared everything they had" (v. 44 NLT) and getting hives at the idea of such an open way of community. I mean, when someone comes to my house without notice, my mouth says "I am glad to see you" while my brain tries to remember if my kids have left underwear on the bathroom floor!

Acts 2 is a depiction of thriving community—between God and His people, His people and one another, and His people and the world. At the beginning of the chapter, we find a bustling Jerusalem with Jews from a myriad of countries gathered together to celebrate a temple feast. They were together for a single purpose, but they were also so different—just consider the unique journeys they took to get there, the diverse styles of dress they donned, the different dialects they spoke, and the varied ages and social classes they represented. It was like those who prefer Chicago-style pizza and those who like New York–style pizza enjoying lunch together! The only thing more amazing than this menagerie of people is the miracle that God did in their midst. These diverse people were transformed by the Spirit of God into one body. He connected three thousand new believers and fused them with the already-existing followers of Jesus to form His church.

In that one day, strangers became neighbors as many of the new believers stayed in that region to start a new life there after their conversion. Those strangers had to grapple with how to live, serve, and commune together while keeping peace, which is no easy trick. They also needed to refrain from placing stumbling blocks in one another's way and judging one another. They ate together, shared ideas, merged jour-neys, gave to the poor, worshiped, grappled with new faith in Christ, and created an example of community that still inspires today. But this amazing unity among believers was fairly short-lived. You see, Acts 2 was written in AD 90 while Romans 14 was written somewhere in the third century; so according to biblical scholars, only about 150–200 years separated them—not a long time in the grand scheme of things.

When the apostle Paul penned Romans 14:13, he was writing to believers like the ones in Acts 2, urging them, "Therefore let us stop passing judgment on one another. Instead, make up your mind not to put any stumbling block or obstacle in the way of a brother or sister." Clearly, he recognized that passing judgment was a common problem

among believers and something of which he himself was guilty: "Let *us* stop." So although he saw the issue as communal, he saw the solution as an individual decision: "Make up *your* mind." He also reminded the believers of their connection to one another, warning against hindering "a brother or sister."

We are made for community and have a responsibility to not undermine one another.

Review Acts 2:42-47 once more and make a list of the attributes of this new group of believers:

How is this first church different from the church you attend?

What is similar about them?

Are there people in your sphere of influence whom you have chosen not to reach out to in the name of Christ because of your concerns about how different they are from you? If so, write about your concerns briefly:

One of the challenges of community is the varying personalities, experiences, backgrounds, perspectives, opinions, strengths, weaknesses, and choices it brings. It is easy to fall into the trap of judging others who are different from us, a trap that undermines true community.

We can see the uniting character of God in Acts 2 as He brought people from different cultures and languages together to make them stronger. We were made for community, and community was made for us. Let us overcome the temptation to judge others and, instead, make sure that we do not create a "stumbling block" with our self-importance. Community is only possible when we recognize that the word *unity* has an "I" right in the middle of it. I must desire biblical unity and work for it to occur. It starts with each of us recognizing that it is our personal responsibility and calling to foster unity by putting pride aside, focusing on what we have in common, and celebrating those things that make us different.

Call to Action

- Invite some people over for a simple meal. Enjoy one another's company for the evening. Share prayer requests and pray for one another. Maybe even schedule another night to get together and follow up on the prayer requests.
- Ask God to show you ways you might be putting an obstacle in the way of a brother or sister in Christ. Pray for forgiveness.
- Revisit your friend list from Day 1 (page 14). Is there anyone on that list you are guilty of judging? If so, consider how your judgment might be a stumbling block to that person, or an obstacle in developing a deeper, more meaningful relationship with that person.

Day 3: Battle Scars (Sitting with Others in the Midst of Pain)

Today's "One Another"

Finally, brothers and sisters, rejoice! Strive for full restoration, encourage one another, be of one mind, live in peace. And the God of love and peace will be with you.

(2 Corinthians 13:11)

I have always been jealous of those women on television who are portrayed as perfect when they wake up in the morning. Their hair is perfectly coiffed and their lip gloss is on point, even if the characters they play have been in a coma for three years. When I wake up, my curly tresses look as if they were in a mixed martial arts battle against one another in the night, and my lips are glossed with slobber!

We all have things about ourselves that we do not like. For some of us, it is our weight. For some, our noses are too small or too big. For some, it's our height, our posture, or the fact that our upper arms hang lower than they once did when we hold them out. I have quite a few things on the list, but none is so pronounced as my disdain from the scars I have earned through two C-sections. The scars are not so ugly themselves; it's the way such a scar misshapes the flesh around it. I'm very self-conscious of it and, frankly, would go so far as to say that I truly hate those scars.

That being said, I could not be more thankful for the human beings who came from those surgeries. They are worth every stitch and staple.

Scars can be difficult and uncomfortable for us. They are reminders of past pain. They often tell stories, and sometimes we are not comfortable with the stories they tell.

Recently, I came across a story that took place at a church not far from my home. A group of five believers had struggled with anxiety for years. One from their group became so desperate and overwhelmed that she attempted suicide. Fortunately, she was not successful. But she had the scars on her wrist as a constant reminder of her anguish.

After hearing a particularly encouraging sermon series on joy based on Philippians 4:4, she had the word *rejoice* tattooed over her scars as a reminder of God's work in her life and the joy she could experience because of it. She wanted the tattoo to serve as a symbol of God's faithfulness—a reminder of her story from a painful season.

But that is not where the story ends. You see, her five friends did the same! They all had a matching tattoo of the word *rejoice* inscribed on their wrists to remind them of her story as well.[3]

When we are in a place of pain, regret, and disappointment, we need people who care for us enough to come alongside us and encourage us, empathize with us, and remind us of the joy available to us in Jesus.

Do you have any physical scars? If so, how did you "earn" them?

What about invisible scars caused by relational wounds? Name one.

What did you learn from that season?

What was your experience of community like during that time?

Many of us misconstrue what community means. Community is not an interpersonal buffet line where we get to pick and choose those in our biblical community. We are called to love our brothers and sisters in Christ even when they are wounded or different or their stories make us feel uncomfortable—or when our story makes *them* uncomfortable.

I am busy. I have three jobs, two kids, a cute husband who cannot pick up his socks, and a church I love. I have a grocery list for every store at which we shop (seriously, every store!) because I want to make sure I get out of the store exactly what I need. The problem is, I take the same posture when it comes to people in my life. When forming a group, making a guest list for a party, or inviting others over for coffee, I often pick those folks who are "the path of least resistance" as friends. I just

want to make sure that our time together is beneficial and a good use of my time and resources—in other words, that it meets my needs and is convenient for me. Even as I am typing this, I know that my perspective, albeit honest, does *not* line up with Scripture. Ouch.

There were a whole lot of Is, *mes*, and *mys* in the last paragraph. The missing pronouns include *they*, *them*, and most important, H*im*.

Even though I am a Christian speaker and should know better, some-times I grow impatient when someone takes too long sharing a prayer request or doesn't tackle problems the way I think they should, instead of empathizing and showing the love of Jesus to those who are hurting, as I should. How about you?

It's easy to suffer from a major case of the *mes*, isn't it? Today's Scripture Focus serves as a great litmus test for selfishness.

Read Proverbs 18:1-2 in the margin and answer the following:

What are we not to do?

What, then, shall we do?

¹Whoever isolates himself seeks his own desire; he breaks out against all sound judgment. ²A fool takes no pleasure in understanding, but only in expressing his opinion. (Proverbs 18:1-2 ESV)

Tucked within these verses in the Old Testament is a reminder to make room for others and their needs, offering understanding. In the New Testament, Jesus brings to light the contrast of our selfishness—which puts a division between us and the community we are designed for—and the unity He desires for us:

²⁰"I do not ask for these only, but also for those who will believe in me through their word, ²¹that they may all be one, just as you, Father, are in me, and I in you, that they also may be in us, so that the world may believe that you have sent me."

(John 17:20-21 ESV)

Although Jesus does not talk about selfishness directly in these passages, it is clear that His desire is for us to be one in Him, which requires empathy and understanding.

The apostle Paul also instructs us about unity and restoration, two opponents of selfishness, in two different letters:

¹⁷I appeal to you, brothers, to watch out for those who cause divisions and create obstacles contrary to the doctrine that you have been taught; avoid them. ¹⁸For such persons do not serve our Lord Christ, but their own appetites, and by smooth talk and flattery they deceive the hearts of the naive.

(Romans 16:17-18 ESV)

¹¹Finally, brothers and sisters, rejoice! Strive for full restoration, encourage one another, be of one mind, live in peace. And the God of love and peace will be with you.

¹²Greet one another with a holy kiss. ¹³All God's people here send their greetings.

¹⁴May the grace of the Lord Jesus Christ, and the love of God, and the fellowship of the Holy Spirit be with you all.

(2 Corinthians 13:11-14)

Read 2 Corinthians 13:11-14 above once more, and circle all the verbs (both action and being verbs). What are the keys to biblical community according to these verses?

What is God's job in all of this?

Unlike most of the letters written by Paul, his Second Letter to the Corinthians ends a bit abruptly. Although he gives really practical advice, he does not beat around the proverbial bush! He simply instructs them to encourage one another and then asks God to bless them.

The church in Corinth is struggling with quarreling and infighting, so Paul reminds them to encourage one another to serve God more effectively. He calls them to community where the differences and experiences of one another need not be a source of arguing or division. Paul is urging them to put their differences aside so they may benefit from the variety of different skills, gifts, and approaches the Body has to offer. His instructions resonate into our lives today, don't they?

In order to accomplish this kind of community, however, we need to find hope in the promise and prayer of this verse: "And the God of love and peace will be with you" (v. 11). Paul knew that it would take more than "playing nice" to bring about mutually meaningful community; he knew it would take the very presence of God. Let's face it: On our own, we are not selfless enough to live at peace with others. Left to our own devices, we might pretend to get along; but without intervention from God, it is no more than a charade.

Finally, in verse 14, Paul offers a blessing that gives us a glimpse into the true community found in the Holy Trinity so that we can follow suit: "May the grace of the Lord Jesus Christ, and the love of God, and the fellowship of the Holy Spirit be with you all."

I want to be the type of person others can trust with their prayer requests, secrets, and scars. I want to be a person who fosters peace, encourages unity, and shows the grace of God in the way I deal with others. I want my relationships to mirror the community found only in the triune God. And I am certain that you do too!

Which of the Scriptures we have looked at today "sticks out" or resonates with you? Why?

When do you find yourself struggling with selfishness? In what area(s) do you find yourself focusing more on your priorities than those of others?

Ask God to show you areas where your selfishness is blocking you from the blessing of unity with others. Make some notes below:

An obstacle to creating and fostering biblical community is our own selfishness. When we want people to conform to our likeness and opinions, we do not grow, nor do we point them toward becoming more like Jesus. If we are going to find our tribe and learn to thrive, we must put our selfish desires aside and trust in the uniting character of God in our life and community. God is bigger than our fears, insecurities, and selfishness. He wants us to grow in our likeness of His Son, but to do so we must recognize where our pride is an obstacle to our growth and to community.

Call to Action

- Make a list of people you know who are hurting. Pick at least one name on the list and brainstorm a creative way to encourage them. Give up an activity this week to make time for connecting with him or her.

Day 4: Building Project

Today's "One Another"

Therefore encourage one another and build each other up, just as in fact you are doing.
(1 Thessalonians 5:11)

Without getting too personal, I would just like to state for the record that I hate bras. They are uncomfortable, frustrating, and, frankly, too expensive for my liking.

I understand their function. I understand the difference they can make, but I hate with a fiery passion the idea of getting fitted for a new one. It is humiliating. It makes me feel vulnerable. It is mortifying.

One day, in the middle of the worship component of our church service, a woman in the congregation whispered in my ear. She was my hairdresser, or as I like to call it, "hairapist." I was lost in the song, overcome by the Spirit with my hands high in the air, when I heard her whisper, "Your bra does not fit properly."

I did not dignify her comment with a response. Instead, I went back to trying to focus on the love of Jesus. It was difficult. All I could concentrate on was the fact that she could see my ill-fitting undergarments that, clearly, were distracting her.

When we sat down to listen and learn from the sermon, she passed me a note. "Friends don't let friends wear the wrong bra. I would love to take you to get properly fitted, if you would like."

I took her up on her offer. I had never done more than the trial-and-error method, and I thought the experience might teach me something. Teach me something it did. First of all, the sales clerk measured every conceivable part of my upper body. She handed me a series of bras and asked me to try them on.

Something she did not tell me, however, is that the dressing rooms in this particular retail store had two doors: the door into the dressing room for the customer, and the door into the dressing room for the clerk. In the middle of attempting to shove myself into the bra, from out of nowhere the clerk appeared. I shrieked. I may have lost a little bit of bladder control, too.

But in the end, I left with well-fitting accoutrements *and* the need for therapy.

Biblical community is not about undergarments, but it *is* about "support" (pun intended). It is about being willing to encourage a sister in Christ—just wait until the end of the service to do so!

I also saw the wisdom in her advice once I "tried it on for size" (again, pun intended). I am so thankful that she loved me enough to "build me up" (okay, I will stop).

When was the last time you had an argument or disagreement with someone? Do you recall the issue? How did it resolve?

²Make my joy complete by being like-minded, having the same love, being one in spirit and of one mind. ³Do nothing out of selfish ambition or vain conceit. (Philippians 2:2-3)

Read Philippians 2:2-3 in the margin. What does *like-minded* mean, in your own words?

Is there someone in your life with whom you are like-minded?

People often misconstrue what *like-minded* means, thinking it is a perpetual "kum bah ya" mindset of meek individuals who lose their own opinions in the stew of discussion.

Instead, like-mindedness for Christians is really about maintaining the purpose of making disciples and keeping that as our unified goal. We all bring different approaches, personalities, experiences, and gifts to the table; but as long as we keep our purpose of sharing the good news of Jesus Christ in sight, we can be like-minded.

The apostle Paul talks about this in terms of "being one in spirit and of one mind" without selfishness or vanity. Paul should know. He had

been a powerful and ruthless persecutor of the church before his conversion; believers were still filled with trepidation at the sound of his name. In Acts 9:26-27, we see that Barnabas had to persuade other believers to allow Paul to participate in fellowship.

Paul and Barnabas became friends and ministry partners after that, and things were good until the two men had a disagreement over another follower, John Mark, a cousin of Barnabas (Colossians 4:10). John Mark joined them on a missionary journey but then left them for home for an unspecified reason (Acts 13:13). When Barnabas later suggested him as a ministry partner for another journey, the disagreement that followed was dramatic indeed. We read about it in Acts 15:

> ³⁶Some time later Paul said to Barnabas, "Let us go back and visit the believers in all the towns where we preached the word of the Lord and see how they are doing." ³⁷Barnabas wanted to take John, also called Mark, with them, ³⁸but Paul did not think it wise to take him, because he had deserted them in Pamphylia and had not continued with them in the work. ³⁹They had such a sharp disagreement that they parted company. Barnabas took Mark and sailed for Cyprus, ⁴⁰but Paul chose Silas and left, commended by the believers to the grace of the Lord. ⁴¹He went through Syria and Cilicia, strengthening the churches.
>
> (Acts 15:36-41)

Why did Paul not want to take Mark on another journey with them? (v. 38)

What happened as a result of Paul and Barnabas's disagreement? (vv. 39-40)

There is no biblical record of Paul and Barnabas ever seeing each other again, though we cannot know for sure whether they did or not.

If you are anything like me, I am curious as to who was right in this scenario. The truth is, these two men of God were not having a doctrinal or theological battle but, instead, a battle over opinion. Paul was guided by his logic and history with Mark—Mark had left another missionary trip early. Barnabas, called the Encourager, was quick to assume the best about Mark and wanted to give him another chance.

I relate to Barnabas. I am so thankful for all of the second chances God has given to me that I, too, am quick to empathize and give second chances to others. Sometimes I even cast logic or common sense aside to do so.

Lloyd Ogilvie wrote: "Paul had fought and won one of history's most crucial battles over the Gentile converts. He was not able, however, to apply the same truth to his relationship with John Mark."[4] The same men who worked so powerfully together to foster community in the body of Christ broke community with each other over a difference of opinion. Fortunately, that is not how the story ends.

In Acts 15:40, Paul and his new ministry partner, Silas, are commended for their faithful work, and years later Paul calls Mark "useful" (2 Timothy 4:11 ESV). In addition, Mark is commended for his service to the church in Colossae (Colossians 4:10).

What can we learn from all this? First, we can glean that sometimes, even with godly people, there is conflict. Fortunately, neither Paul nor Barnabas stopped doing ministry or spreading the gospel. When we have a disagreement with a brother or sister in Christ, it should not deter us from fulfilling our purpose: to love God and others. Paul certainly was not deterred from his call to do so by sharing the good news.

Luke, the writer of Acts, was led by the Holy Spirit to chronicle this incident, even though it could have been terribly embarrassing to his good friend Paul. This account of this personal conflict plays an important role in acknowledging the challenges of biblical community. Even leaders such as Paul and Barnabas were not exempt from conflict. Paul even mentions Barnabas in a respectful way (1 Corinthians 9:6), which might indicate a softening toward his old friend, though we cannot know for sure.

Second, God used this rift between these two men to create two teams for ministry—to spread the good news of Jesus.

How do you think Paul and Barnabas might have been shaped by their disagreement? (There are no right or wrong answers here.)

Paul, led by the Spirit of God, penned our "one another" verse of the day: "Therefore encourage one another and build each other up, just as in fact you are doing" (1 Thessalonians 5:11). I wonder if he had Barnabas, the Encourager, in mind when he wrote it.

What can we learn from disagreements with others? Share an example from your own life, if possible.

How has God shaped your view of others, yourself, and Him through disagreements?

Let us remember that even in our disagreements, brokenness, selfishness, and scars, God is still in control and can use it to bring good. What a relief!

Call to Action

- Review an area of your life where God has shaped you through a disagreement. Did it erode your selfishness and pride? Ask God to show you how He has used it to make you stronger or better.
- Biblical community is made up of imperfect people with imperfect problems. If we are to forge true friendships—those built on Jesus and His love for us—we must be willing to encourage others, even those with whom we do not agree.

Identify two people you can encourage this week, including someone with whom you do not agree.

- When there is conflict—and there will always be conflict in authentic relationships—we must be willing to pray for, support, and build up the other. Pray for someone with whom you are in conflict or have been in conflict in the past.

Day 5: Clean Shave

Today's "One Another"

Scripture Focus

Genesis 2:18-25

And let us consider how we may spur one another on toward love and good deeds.

(Hebrews 10:24)

I taught junior high for many years. My prayer was always that my students would learn a lot, but often I would glean more from them than they from me. One particular year, one of the girls in my class, I will call her Sally, was struck with alopecia. Alopecia is a common autoimmune disorder that often results in unpredictable hair loss. According to Medical News Today, it affects roughly 6.8 million people in the United States.[5] But when one is in junior high, it doesn't really matter how many other people it affects; you just know that it affects you. I am confident that, since no one else in our school had such a medical condition, she must have felt terribly lonely and isolated.

For many people with alopecia, hair falls out in small patches all around their head in areas about the size of a quarter. For most, it is just a few patches; for Sally, it was greater than that. It was so extreme that she eventually acquiesced and shaved her whole head; she thought it was easier than to try to manage the myriad of patches all around her head. The day that she came to school without any hair was a bit shocking. By this time, it was not just the hair on her head that was gone; she also had lost her eyebrows. None of us knew what to do. None of us knew what to say or how to say it other than "I'm praying for you."

When I was that age, it was the mid 1980s. My hair was so big and fluffy that it received a radio signal. I took great pride in securing every hair in place with enough hairspray to cause an environmental crisis. My hair was part of my identity. I cannot imagine losing my hair at that age.

But the girls in Sally's class had an idea. It was a private school, and so classes were small in size. They were an especially tight-knit group, and they proved their closeness this particular year. During the most awkward and crazy time in one's development, all of these girls shaved their heads to support Sally. They decided that if she had to go through something so terrible, they would not allow her to do it by herself. When they entered the class, shiny heads and all, I could not hold back the tears. I was so blessed by these girls who chose to show this young woman that she, indeed, was loved and supported; they chose to truly empathize with a friend in pain. I was convicted. Although I did not shave my head, I was forever changed by their gesture. And I know Sally was as well—even long after her hair grew back.

Have you ever felt lonely and isolated? If so, describe how you felt:

What do you do when you feel disconnected from others? from God?

Loneliness is no joke. As we discussed earlier in the week, we were created in the image of God, and He exists in perfect community—Father, Son, and Holy Spirit. But we do not exist in perfect community. We are imperfect. The people in our lives are imperfect. In the story of Creation, there was only one thing that was labeled "not good."

Read Genesis 2:18 in the margin. What did God say was "not good"?

The Lord God said, "It is not good for the man to be alone. I will make a helper suitable for him."
(Genesis 2:18)

God said that it was not good for man to be alone. So God remedied the situation by creating a suitable helper for man, creating the first biblical community between two humans.

When we do not have community, loneliness is a natural by-product. We are designed for connection with others.

Before Adam and Eve ate the forbidden fruit, loneliness did not exist. Adam and Eve had perfect community with each other and with God. They walked around wearing nothing but smiles (literally); although they were completely vulnerable, they were completely safe. They wore their birthday suits every day—and it was not even their birthday!

And then they ate the fruit. In doing so, they broke perfect community with God.

Read Genesis 3:1-12. How do we know that Adam and Eve's communion with God was broken? (v. 8)

What did Adam say when God questioned him about eating the forbidden fruit? (v. 12)

When God confronted Adam, Adam immediately pointed a finger at Eve, breaking perfect community with his wife and separating himself from her. Disconnection occurred.

I would have bet money on the fact that the first disconnection between man and wife would have been over the remote control, but I was wrong.

Loneliness was certainly not what God designed for His people, but loneliness can remind us to seek the face of God. God is a God of restoration, and he can redeem our loneliness and disconnection and draw us to Himself. We might think of loneliness as a "warning light," reminding us to draw near to God. Not only can loneliness point us to our need

to draw close to God but it also can serve as a reminder that we should encourage others to do likewise—just as Today's "One Another" verse reminds us.

Read Hebrews 10:24 again:

"And let us consider how we may spur one another on toward love and good deeds."

Who is to consider? Circle the pronoun.

What are we to consider? Underline the answer.

The verse begins with community: "And let *us* consider. . . ." The action, "spur one another on," also encourages community, and the phrase "toward love and good deeds" specifically promotes community that honors God. This verse is both a cure for loneliness and a call to community.

What mental pictures come to mind when you think of "spurring"?

Why do you think this word was used regarding the concept of community?

When was the last time you felt encouraged by a brother or sister in Christ?

When was the last time you went out of your way to encourage another?

Today's verse is kicked off with the words *and let*. The verb "let" communicates that in order to spur another on, we must first submit to God how we consider or view the responsibility He has given us. To "let" suggests a choice and a surrender. We have to acquiesce to what God is calling us to and trust that spurring makes everyone better. Spurring is designed to get attention and promote action and movement. We must also see those around us in biblical community as conduits of growth in our lives, which may indeed involve spurring of sorts. Spurring may not always feel good, but it keeps us moving forward.

Call to Action

- Contact your church office to find the contact information for some shut-ins in your area. Write each one a card, reminding them that they are loved and valuable. Let them know that they are not alone.
- Write a letter to a friend, thanking her or him for the friendship you share and encouraging her or him to keep up the good work!
- Think of someone that might need some "spurring." Perhaps a person you have not seen at church lately could use some encouragement to return, or someone who is hesitant to use her gifting might benefit from your support and accountability.

Weekly Wrap-up

This week our theme has been finding one another, which has to do with friendship through the lens of biblical community. When we are in true friendship with someone else, it is a mutually beneficial arrangement. But friendship is not without its challenges. In the Word of God we are commanded to (among other things) be devoted to one

another, honor one another, stop passing judgment on one another, encourage one another, be of one mind, build each other up, and spur one another on toward love and good deeds. Throughout the week, we've explored these one anothers along with some truths regarding biblical community:

we were created by God for community;
we need community;
there is risk involved in community, but there is also reward.

We looked at Acts 2 for insight on what community should look like and how God can unite His people despite our many differences and our selfishness. Finally, we explored our responsibilities in biblical community and how we might foster healthy and mutually beneficial community that brings praise to God.

The Sandbox of Biblical Community

Here's a helpful metaphor to keep in mind throughout our study. Friendship in biblical community is like the sandbox many of us played in when we were children. As we shoveled sand alongside others, we learned about sharing space and conflict resolution (not to mention the ramifications of eating sand), gained the skills to build and plan, and gleaned how to share the box with others who were at different stages of development. Often, much to my dismay, I had to learn to share my shovel, bucket, and plastic rake—the tools of the sandbox—with others.

Similarly, the sandbox of biblical community is where we learn to learn and grow with other believers. We can learn more each day about how God is shaping us and the people around us to be more like Him. But we will need to live it out as we share, resolve conflict fairly and peaceably, and have empathy for those who are at different stages in their spiritual development. We also need to accept grace and love from those who have had more time in the sandbox of faith. As we begin to "share the tools" of the sandbox with joy, we come to realize that it is an honor to grow alongside sisters and brothers in the faith.

Every project involves goals, which help us to chart our way toward the desired objective. The Belonging Project is no different. Now that we have uncovered the value of biblical community, let's take some time to think about some goals that will help to move us toward that objective.

When making goals, whether in business or in our personal and spiritual lives, the S.M.A.R.T. framework can help us ensure success. Each goal should meet the SMART criteria:

Specific	What exactly is your goal? Instead of "I want friends," consider a specific goal, such as saying, "I will be intentional about connecting with others three days each week."
Measureable	What will you see, feel, hear, and experience when you reach your goal? For example, will you have coffee with one friend a week?
Attainable	Is it a realistic goal? Do you have either the time, talent, money, or capacity, or all of these, to make it happen? Though you want to leave "God space" in your goals—so that your goal is bigger than yourself and you rely on God for strength—you never want to set a goal that will end up discouraging you.
Relevant	Why do you want to reach this goal? Why does it matter?
Timely	What is the deadline for this goal?

I want to encourage you to begin your journey of "finding your tribe and learning to thrive" by setting a few personal goals.

After praying about it, write one or two S.M.A.R.T. goals related to community:

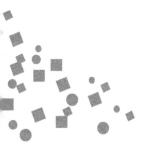

Find One Another

Friendship Through the Lens
of Biblical Community

We were created for community, a place where we can be vulnerable, encourage one another, and thrive.

Welcome/Prayer/Icebreaker (5–10 minutes)

Welcome to Session 1 of The Belonging Project: Finding Your Tribe and Learning to Thrive. Over the next four weeks we're going to discover how to live a life in community that is both fun and fulfilling by examining some of the "one another" phrases in the New Testament. This week we've explored how we are meant for connection, not disconnection, and how we can "find one another" through true biblical friendship. Today we're exploring what that kind of community and connection look like.

Take a moment to open with prayer, and then go around the circle and share one or two attributes that you look for in a friend.

Video (about 20 minutes)

Play the video segment for Week 1, filling in the blanks as you watch and making notes about anything that resonates with you or that you want to be sure to remember.

—Video Notes—

Scripture Focus: Romans 12:9-10

H _____

"[Love must] be _____." (Romans 12:9)

H _____ _____

"Hold fast to what is _____." (Romans 12:9 ESV)

H _____

"Love one another with brotherly _____." (Romans 12:10 ESV)

H _____

"Outdo one another in showing _____." (Romans 12:10 ESV)

Other Insights:

Group Discussion (20–25 minutes for a 60-minute session; 30–35 minutes for a 90-minute session)

Video Discussion

- What do you think it means to be a "connector" for God?
- In our world of carefully crafted identities and personas, what can it mean to love others genuinely?
- How has the structure of community (or lack of) with other believers affected your life?
- What should brotherly/sisterly love look like within the community of Christ?

Workbook Discussion

- What are some specific ways you have both shown and received devotion and honor in relationships? (page 15)
- In Genesis 12, we see God asking Abram to give up all he knows and start over again. When have you had to start over again? How did you react, and what did you gain from that risk?
- Read Romans 14:13 aloud. What does it mean to "stop passing judgment on one another"? How is that different from pointing out something about which someone is wrong? (page 21)
- What is your response to the description of this community of early believers in Acts 2:42-47? (page 21)
- According to 2 Corinthians 13:11-14, what are the keys to biblical community? What is God's job? What is our job? (pages 28-29)
- What can we learn from disagreements with others? Share an example from your own life, if possible. (page 35)
- When was the last time you felt encouraged by a brother or sister in Christ? When was the last time you went out of your way to encourage another? (pages 39-40)
- What are your hopes or expectations for finding and thriving in biblical community?

Connection Point (10–15 minutes—90-minute session only)

Divide into groups of two to three and discuss the following:

- What do you do when you feel disconnected from others? from God? (page 37)
- How is God prompting you to think or live differently as a result of what you've heard or learned this week?

Closing Prayer (5 minutes)

Close the session by sharing personal prayer requests and praying together. If you like, invite the women to surround those who have shared requests and pray for them aloud. In addition to praying aloud for one another, close by asking God to help you be a biblical connector, following Jesus's lead in honoring and loving others, and by asking Him to guide you in finding true biblical community.

Week 2

Fellowship with One Another

Deeper Connection Through the Lens of Biblical Community

Memory Verse

Now that you have purified yourselves by obeying the truth so that you have sincere love for each other, love one another deeply, from the heart.

(1 Peter 1:22)

Day 1: Friendly Reminder

Scripture Focus

Romans 1:28-30;
2 Corinthians 12:20

Today's "One Another"

Brothers and sisters, do not slander one another. Anyone who speaks against a brother or sister or judges them speaks against the law and judges it. When you judge the law, you are not keeping it, but sitting in judgment on it.

(James 4:11)

I love God's Word. I love the wisdom, encouragement, life, and power it provides me. I love the way it both corrects and edifies me. Some verses, however, are easier to understand than others.

When I was in Bible college, I was blessed with a fantastic group of roommates. My favorite roommate, Charity, was a true gift from God. She had been raised in a Christian home, the daughter of a pastor, and practiced wonderful spiritual habits from which I could learn. One of these included a very regular quiet time; she taught me the strength we can draw from a regular time in God's Word and in prayer. She was a wonderful example. In addition, she modeled for me how to be a true friend and faithful prayer supporter.

We had different school and work schedules, so sometimes, when we did not see each other for a day or so, we would encourage each other with a Scripture that had been particularly meaningful to us.

She would put a sticky note with a verse on it and post it on the bathroom mirror that we shared. It was a gift each time not only to read the verse she had shared but also to get a glimpse of the things with which she might be struggling or grappling.

I remember the day that the note she left for me had a plethora of stars all over it. This had never occurred before. I knew this was going to be a major verse. Not that all Scripture verses are not "major" in importance, but the way that she took the time to really emphasize it meant that this was going to be a glimpse into her soul. I knew it would serve to encourage me. When I looked up the verse she had penned on the note, it read: "Do not cook a young goat in its mother's milk" (Exodus 23:19).

Wow. I didn't know what to say. If Charity was sharing her heart with me, I was not getting the message. Instead, I was given a "recipe warning" for the people of Israel!

When I saw Charity next, I gingerly asked about the verse. I did not want to admit that I did not understand the significance of the verse, so I tried to figure it out through inquiry. "What exactly was striking to you about this particular verse and what made it star-worthy?" I asked.

What followed was an impressive string of theological and philosophical commentaries, but then she grinned and said, "I can't do it; I can't hold my laughter back any longer. I did it as a joke. I just thought it would be hilarious. I envisioned you running to your Bible and being shocked at what you found. "

Shocked I was, and puzzled. I know every verse in the Bible has purpose—to help us understand God more clearly and teach us more about who He is, how to be more like Him, and how to better love one another, which is our focus this week. But some verses are easier to understand than others, right?

That's one reason I love the Book of James (which is, by far, my favorite book of the Bible); it is straightforward with practical charges throughout. One such charge is found in Today's "One Another" verse. No need for guessing games here! This verse speaks to us about a behavior that not only destroys relationships but also can damage the fellowship of the larger community.

James 4:11 begins, "Brothers and sisters." I think it's interesting that, in the formation of this verse, the Holy Spirit had James start with the reminder of who we are. He reminds us that we are brothers and sisters in Christ and should act accordingly. We are family, in the most healthy sense of the word, and our actions should reflect who our Father is and the things He has taught us. In fact, when we, as brothers and sisters in Christ, recognize who we are in Him and His love for us, we *naturally* want to share that love with others.

James quickly goes on to command us, "do not slander one another." The root word for *slander* is much like the term *backbite*. In other words, we are not to make damaging statements about others behind their backs. This does not reflect the love of the Father.

Has another person ever made damaging statements about you behind your back? If so, briefly tell what happened:

Have you ever made damaging statements about another person behind his or her back? What effect did your comments have?

The only other times the apostle Paul uses this word are in Romans 1:28-30 and 2 Corinthians 12:20, and neither instance is complimentary. In his Letter to the Romans, Paul addresses the characteristics of a group of people who had completely turned their backs on God and His love.

Read Romans 1:28-30 and list all of the characteristics Paul names in these verses:

This is a hearty list to describe those outside of the teachings of Christ.

In his second letter to the church in Corinth, Paul does not list the characteristics of those outside the love of God but the characteristics of a church who has not adhered to the teachings and example of Christ.

Read 2 Corinthians 12:20, and once again list the characteristics Paul names:

This is a pointed reminder of how far we can get off track as believers when our faith is not placed firmly in Christ but in our own desires and importance.

Now circle the word *slander* in the two previous lists.

Clearly, slander is not fitting for a follower of Jesus and is not conducive to the loving community and connection He desires for us.

James continues, "Anyone who speaks against a brother or sister or judges them speaks against the law and judges it." These words clarify that speaking against a brother or sister undermines the love we are supposed to show them. They also remind us not to judge; *judging*, in this case, is not the same as the discernment that comes when someone is not adhering to the teachings of Christ. Pointing out sin in a brother or sister, *when done in love*, is healthy. What James is talking about here is not sin issues but preference issues—judging others for having different opinions or practices that God allows. Maybe they listen to music you find unsavory. Maybe they belong to a political party with which you disagree. Maybe their denomination is different from yours.

Matthew 7:1 addresses the same concept: "Do not judge, or you too will be judged." To make one's opinion more important than the true laws of God is worthy of judgment. I do not know about you, but I do not want to be accused of judging the validity of the very Word of God and its teachings. As James concludes in verse 11, "When you judge the law, you are not keeping it, but sitting in judgment on it."

Jesus spent a lot of time loving people while on earth, but he also spent time rebuking those who added their own preferences to the Law through religion. The religious leaders of the day would add extraneous requirements, or shackles, to the people, and the burden of these shackles separated them from God.

Like the religious leaders rebuked by Jesus, if you and I spend time judging and backbiting a fellow believer, we are not only disobeying the commands of God; we are standing in opposition of them and, therefore, deserving of judgment or accountability.

But it happens all the time, doesn't it? Judgment between people who claim to know Christ happens in Facebook posts, on social media forums, and in women's ministry committee meetings. It happens in coffee shops, in church hallways, and in our hearts.

When we judge others, it shows our lack of faith in God's fairness and goodness.

> **A common accusation of nonbelievers is that Christians are judgmental. Have you ever found that to be a valid accusation in a particular instance? If so, explain your response.**

> **Judging and praying both require self-examination. If we find ourselves judging others, how might we humble ourselves through prayer?**

When driving, I often feel nervous at the sight of a police car behind me, even when I am not breaking the law. I am certain he or she will find something terribly wrong with my driving, and so I check my speedometer a hundred times, use the turn signal 187 feet before I need to do so, and am no fun for the people riding in my car at the time.

When we judge others, they feel they are in social and spiritual "traffic" with a patrol car following them. We do not want to be the ones judging their performance or journey; that is God's job. We will thwart biblical community if people feel judged by us. Let us commit to trust

God to do His job as righteous Judge and loving Father—in equal parts truth and grace.

Call to Action

- Make a list of people you find yourself judging. Pray for them by name out loud and ask for forgiveness.
- If we are going to thrive in biblical community, we must own up to the things we do that separate us from one another and from God. We must be willing to share both our strengths and our weaknesses and set aside judgments against others. Identify a judgment you've made that you need to set aside today.

Day 2: Mat Mates

Scripture Focus

Luke 5:17-26

Today's "One Another"

Don't grumble against one another, brothers and sisters, or you will be judged. The Judge is standing at the door!

(James 5:9)

Recently while speaking at an event that included numerous presenters, I met a delightful woman who has authored many books and has faithfully encouraged women in their walk with Christ for many years. As we spoke, we discovered that we had lived in the same area at different times. Although she is a bit older than I, we had many mutual friends. When I asked about all the opportunities she had had to speak, she listed many of the organizations and churches where I have wanted to speak for years—decades, actually. The envy began to gnaw at me. She has walked through ministry doors that have been closed to me.

I maintained my smile, but I started an internal grumbling. I grumbled about all the opportunities that she had that I didn't. I grumbled about her husband's successful church ministry and how it undoubtedly bolstered her success. I even grumbled about the many hardships she has endured because it gave her a more dramatic platform on which to tell others of the grace of God. I thought her accomplishments were a source of pride for her, so I grumbled at the injustice of it all (ah, the irony!).

Grumblings are the negative words that we murmur either under our breath or in our spirit, but they illustrate a lack of trust in God and how He works. We often grumble about unfairness—about what He has given others but not us. Our circumstances. Our hardships.

Later that evening, when we were by ourselves in the dressing room, I asked for her forgiveness. Through tears, I admitted that my envy disallowed me to hear her message clearly that evening—a message I clearly needed to hear. I also confessed that it was I who struggled with pride, not her.

She was more than gracious. She was humble. She not only forgave me, she prayed for me. How frustrating is that! When I admitted what a spiritual worm I had been, she had the audacity to encourage me and point me to Jesus! I am so excited to say that we still tour together periodically, and I love learning from her. If I had stayed in my grumbling state, I would have missed out on an immense blessing.

Is grumbling something you ever struggle with?

_____ **Never** _____ **Rarely** _____ **Sometimes**

_____ **Often** _____ **All the time**

What characteristics do you equate with those who grumble?

Who in your life is a grumbler? What do they grumble about? Does it make you more or less likely to share things with them?

When my sister got married, one of her closest friends at the time—I will call her Jennifer—offered to take all of her wedding photos as a gift. I can say with honesty that wedding photography in those days, pre-Pinterest, was not the art form it is now, but it is still a chronicle of one of the most important days in a couple's life. Jennifer walked around and took numerous photos throughout the day. It was a glorious wedding, and I do not remember my sister ever looking so radiant, so beautiful.

My sister was married long before digital cameras, so Jennifer's camera was a film camera, and there was no way to know how the photos would look until they were developed. Now, you may be too young to remember a time when film was developed, and if so, I will refrain from making sarcastic comments. The film was taken into a dark room, creatively called a "darkroom," where it was mixed with chemicals and hung to dry as the photos developed. During that process, one-third of every picture Jennifer had taken did not develop; they were totally without color or image. One-third of every photo she took were solid black. I'm not sure we ever uncovered exactly what was wrong with the camera, but you can imagine my sister's dismay when all of the film was developed.

There was no way to re-create that wedding day and recapture the events that were photographed. In some cases, the top third of the photo was black and the heads of the wedding guests were decapitated. In other cases, if there were three people in the picture, the person on the left was completely cut off. In some, the bottom third of the photo was black. Even the full-length view of my sister and her beautiful dress did not turn out.

The problem with our grumbling is that often we do not see the whole picture. We, as finite beings, can only see incomplete pictures. We cannot possibly understand the whole picture that the infinite God sees when He makes His plans. We may see a portion of the picture, but in no way does that allow us or give us the right to grumble.

Even if we don't grumble out loud, but instead are complaining in our spirits and not talking to God or the other person involved about it, we are in sin. Our "one another" of the day, James 5:9, begins, "Don't grumble against one another, brothers and sisters." When a brother or sister in Christ does something that hurts or offends us, we have a responsibility to go to that person directly.

Read Matthew 18:15-19. How do these verses instruct us to handle conflict?

These verses remind us that in order to live in healthy biblical community, we must be honest with one another. We may not think of this as a spiritual issue, but it absolutely is.

We do not have a full picture of all that is happening with others, of all that our sisters and brothers are going through. However, it is our responsibility to support one another and not grumble. And if compassion alone is not sufficient motivation, the next part of James 5:9 might give us pause: "or you will be judged. The Judge is standing at the door!"

In Revelation 3:20, Jesus gives us a beautiful promise: "Here I am! I stand at the door and knock. If anyone hears my voice and opens the door, I will come in and eat with that person, and they with me." According to this verse, Jesus stands at the door knocking and waiting. But the stark contrast to that is the picture in James 5. Here the Judge is not standing at the door to knock politely; He is standing at the door because we are hurting His body, undermining other people with our inward grumblings. Jesus comes both as Savior and as Judge. He will judge not only the world but also the faithfulness of believers (see 2 Corinthians 5:10). Knowing that our faithfulness will be judged, we should take care to be loving toward others, especially our sisters and brothers in Christ.

What if you and I decided that instead of grumbling when a sister or brother does something in disobedience to God—something that harms themselves, us, or others—we will approach our sister or brother just like the friends who helped their crippled friend in Luke 5?

When I think about Jesus standing at the door of my heart, I cannot help reflecting on my attitude, the way I think about others, and about the ways I do not display God's love accurately. If I am honest, I need to spend more time working in the best interest of others instead of grumbling against them in my heart. In addition, I need to ask God who in my life needs someone to carry them to the feet of Jesus in my prayers.

Read Luke 5:17-26 and answer the following:

What is wrong with the man?

What do the friends do to get him to Jesus?

What "miracle" does Jesus do first?

What miracle does He do after that?

If we view a person's spiritual issue as something that is just as important to be healed as a physical issue, it is not such a far-fetched idea that if someone needs encouragement to turn from him or her sinful choice, then Jesus is the best place for them. What if, instead of standing in our own judgment seat, thinking that we are superior, we love him or her enough to take a sister or brother caught in sin to Jesus? That involves praying for the person, speaking truth to him or her in love, and extending the grace that we have received from Christ.

I think it's so important that James reminds us that the Judge is standing at the door, because when we grumble, we've put ourselves in the Judge's seat. And that is never our seat to occupy. Not only are we not capable of such a task, we are not meant to sit in the Judge's seat because we are unable to be as merciful as Christ.

Have you ever been judged by someone unfairly? If so, how did it feel?

Have you ever confronted someone about something the person was doing that was wrong? Did you have a full picture of the situation when you did so? What happened?

Are you sitting in judgment of someone right now? If so, have you prayed about it? Have you sought the Scriptures for wisdom and guidance about the issue? What is God calling you to do?

Just like the photos of my sister's wedding that were developed in the dark, our faith is often developed in the dark. The process of living in community allows us to glimpse a more complete picture of how God sees us. Being in God's Word brings into focus the things about which God is passionate. Being willing to hold back judgment while speaking the truth in love sharpens the edges of our blurry view of others. If we are going to thrive in community through loving connection, we must choose to allow God to stay on the throne and not try to put ourselves in His place.

When we trust God to be the Judge and focus on His righteousness, not our own, He increases our ability to see others and ourselves more clearly.

Call to Action

- When I am feeling insecure about myself or about my relationship with Jesus, the first thing I lose is perspective about myself. Shortly thereafter, I lose my perspective on others. I often get judgmental about others, when the truth is that I am the one who is at fault.
- Who do you find yourself judging? If it is an individual, strategize a plan to ask for forgiveness. If it is a people group, find a way to do community service for that group. It is possible that when you serve them, you will be given new eyes with which to appreciate them.
- When was the last time you felt judged? How did it make you feel? Journal about that experience and how it has affected (or will affect) your interactions with others.

Day 3: Friend or Foe

Scripture Focus

James 4:6

Today's "One Another"

All of you, clothe yourselves with humility toward one another, because,
  "God opposes the proud
  but shows favor to the humble."

(1 Peter 5:5b)

I am a huge football fan. I know I just lost some of you, but bear with me.

My family watched football when I was a kid. Watching football represents some of the few memories I have of my mom and dad being together because they split when I was young.

My dad and sister were both born in California. My mom and I were both born in Texas. When California football teams would play against Texas teams, we would have a smack talk contest before and cheer like crazy people all game long. Plus, any day that the goal is to snack for four hours with friends and family makes this girl happy!

I loved the Dallas Cowboys from the first time I saw their shiny outfits (I just got some of you back). They seemed to have the happiest cheerleaders, the coolest stadium, and the rowdiest fans (from what I could see on TV). Although most of my family does not love the Cowboys these days, they cannot deter me from my undying devotion. I still love them. Hard.

And I still hate the California football teams. Hate is a strong word, but through most of my childhood, the San Francisco 49ers were my dad's favorite, the Raiders were my sister's favorite, and they both were the rivals of the Cowboys. I know Jesus died for them, too, but I just cannot be swayed to love them because they seem to be enemies of my team.

Ryan Switzer is an NFL player who originally was drafted by the Cowboys and then was traded to the Raiders—and most recently to the Steelers. He is an All-American wide receiver and a force to be reckoned with. I remember when he left the Cowboys, exchanging his silver, blue, and white jersey with a giant star on it for the Raiders' black and silver jersey. Although he was traded, he left with nothing but unkind things to say about his time with my Boys.

It felt personal. He signed with the enemy(ish). It felt like betrayal because he went from friend to foe with one signature.

Name some well-known rivals. They can be cartoon characters, movie stars, or people in the Bible.

Define the word _enemy_.

I do not really have enemies. People who cut me off in traffic, women who look great in jeans, those who blast their music so loud in their cars that the bass thumps my sternum, and those who have perfectly clean homes are not my enemies . . . but I do pray for them.

Seriously, doesn't it seem that so often today we vilify others who are not our true enemies? The solution is found in one simple word: *humility*. Rick Warren defined humility this way: "Humility is not thinking less of yourself, it's thinking of yourself less."[1]

Today's "One Another" verse urges us, "All of you, clothe yourselves with humility toward one another, because, 'God opposes the proud but shows favor to the humble'" (1 Peter 5:5b). This verse hits close to home for me, because although I know I want to be humble, it is an everyday struggle to pray for more of God and less of me. Although this is a challenging verse, when dissected into parts, it offers us hope and instruction in three areas: community, clothing, and character.

This is one of those verses that explicitly includes all believers: "All of you." As we have discussed, we are made in the image of God and for community. This, in my opinion, gives us permission to ask for help, draw strength from one another, and reach out to others in order to fulfill the rest of the verse.

The cool juxtaposition in the phrase "clothe yourself with humility toward one another" is that "yourself" is sandwiched between "all of you" and "toward one another." It does not say "clothe one another" (which would be super awkward!). This is a personal responsibility to choose humility each day, especially in light of one's sisters and brothers.

The final part of the verse, "God opposes the proud but shows favor to the humble," is a quote from Proverbs 3:34. It is clear that God is serious about humility in His people, not because He is unfair or needy, but because humility is what is best for us. The same proverb is mentioned in another verse in the New Testament.

Read James 4:6 in the margin. Based on this verse, what is another word for the favor God shows us when we are humble?

But he gives us more grace. That is why Scripture says: "God opposes the proud but shows favor to the humble."

(James 4:6)

God gives us grace when we humble ourselves, but a lack of humility is in opposition to who God is. Pride is an enemy of God. Just like the enemies we listed earlier, the proud are opposed to the God who made them.

In some people, pride looks like arrogance—boasting, feeling superior, and having a combative spirit. Social media is made for people like this; some people like the anonymity of the Internet to judge others, complain, and post their opinions. In others, it looks like self-reliance or busyness for the sake of self-importance. For some, it looks like humility on the outside, but on the inside there is a deep-seated need for affirmation from others instead of seeking God for fulfillment. In many, it looks like religion instead of a humble relationship with Jesus.

I do not want to allow my actions, feelings, and thoughts to oppose the only One who knows me fully, loves me completely, and died for me sacrificially. But when I put myself first in importance or prioritize what I need over what God has called me to do, that is exactly what I am doing.

Who is the most humble person you know? How does that person show his or her humility?

How does this person's humility affect the people around him or her?

Where do you see pride manifest itself in your life? In what area do you most struggle with pride (not confidence in the Lord but pride that is focused on yourself)?

How do we clothe ourselves with humility? Describe some things we can do.

In what areas do you need to put more faith in God and less in your own abilities?

If we are to clothe ourselves with humility, we need to recognize our need (just think of the vulnerability of nudity!), choose to put it on, and live in it all day. The community to which God has called each of us invites us to follow the example of His Son in love and humility.

Call to Action

- Ask God to show you new ways to be humble. It may be listening to another instead of inserting your opinion. It may be letting others go ahead of you in traffic (even when you have the right-of-way) or in the grocery line. List some simple ways you can show humility in your everyday life.

- Humility in community takes many forms. For some, it is serving behind the scenes. For others, it is giving up a night to babysit for a family with foster kids so that the parents can get some time to reconnect. For others, it is really listening and investing in the life of another. It also can look like relinquishing control to God when He calls us to do something brave. What is one way God is calling you to show humility in community with others?

Day 4: Open House

Today's "One Another

Offer hospitality to one another without grumbling.
(1 Peter 4:9)

Scripture Focus

1 Peter 4:9

Early in our marriage, I wanted to be the perfect wife and the perfect hostess. But then reality set in. We lived in this ridiculously small apartment in Southern California. It had both cockroaches and mice despite everything humanly possible to deter them.

The first people we invited over to our apartment were my in-laws. My mother-in-law had the gift of hospitality in spades. She made everyone feel so important, and she seemed to be able to time everything so perfectly that it looked effortless.

I wanted to impress my new family with a delicious meal and a great time of connection. However, the dinner that I had premade and frozen was not as defrosted as I wanted it to be, and it still had about ten minutes to cook. We had very few minutes before they were to arrive, and I began to panic. I must have pressed the wrong button, for even after twenty-five minutes, the middle section of the dish was cold as a stone. What a disaster!

The next couple to grace our newlywed apartment was the senior pastor and his wife. We attended a church with a very large congregation, and although my husband served on staff, we were too naive to realize how many dinner invitations they must have received each week. However, they graciously accepted our invitation.

Scott and I spent time in prayer before they arrived. We did not pray that God would encourage this couple as we met together. We did not pray that God would be honored in the evening. We prayed that the roaches would stay off the wall while they were there—that the Holy Spirit would keep at bay those disgusting creatures so that they did not gross out our guests.

I thought we were successful. However, right in middle of dessert, I looked past the couple who was facing my husband and me to see a giant cockroach scaling the wall like a Cirque du Soleil performer. I did not know what to do. I did not want to panic or bring attention to it, but I wanted it off my wall and out of my sight!

After dessert was over, my husband sprang into action. He invited the loving couple to see our wedding album, pulled out the photos, and strategically positioned them in chairs with their backs to the creepy critter. I quickly put the bug out of its misery (and mine) and returned to our guests. That night was a bit of a disaster as well. I was so worried about our guests and their opinion of us that I do not remember a single thing about that evening other than the bug situation. I missed out learning from two incredibly godly people because of my desire to practice hospitality.

Our verse of the day reminds us to "offer hospitality to one another without grumbling." I have gotten to a place where I believe I offer hospitality readily, but I still have not nailed the concept of doing it without grumbling or stressing out. Yet the biblical model of hospitality is not about the details and the delicacies but about care for others. In the story of Mary and Martha opening their home to Jesus, Martha stressed out about all the details and the tasks and missed the opportunity to connect with Jesus.

When you think of hospitality, what comes to mind?

Do you consider yourself hospitable? Why or why not?

Why do you think hospitality is important in the life of the Body?

Just because I do not feel like I have the gift of hospitality does not get me off the hook. Today's "One Another" verse is quite pointed in its call for each of us to open our lives to others. Hospitality and fellowship go hand in hand, as the Greek language helps us to see.

Oftentimes, we Christians use Greek words to name vocal groups, Bible studies, and buildings—which was very confusing to me when I first was a believer. It was like some secret handshake that no one out of the "Jesus Club" was privy to. But sometimes the Greek term has more depth than its English counterpart. And I believe that's true for the Greek term for Christian fellowship, which happens to be one of the most popular Greek words, *koinonia*. Here is the definition according to the Merriam-Webster dictionary:

Koinonia. 1 : the Christian fellowship or body of believers.
2 : intimate spiritual communion and participative sharing in a common religious commitment and spiritual community
//the *koinonia* of the disciples with each other and with their Lord[2]

Another Greek word that many biblical scholars associate with koinonia is *agape*. Agape is, in simple terms, "God love." It is loving another unconditionally without the expectation of being loved or appreciated in return. True koinonia requires hospitality and offers agape love, and it is one of the greatest rewards and challenges of following Jesus. We need it, we were created for it, and our faith is strengthened by it.

As we discover in the Beatitudes, agape love extends beyond our neighbor.

> **Read Matthew 5:43-45 in the margin. Besides our neighbor, whom are we to love?**

[43]You have heard that it was said, "Love your neighbor and hate your enemy." [44]But I tell you, love your enemies and pray for those who persecute you, [45]that you may be children of your Father in heaven. (Matthew 5:43-45)

Wow. My enemy? If agape love requires me to love my enemy, and agape love includes showing hospitality, then I am to show hospitality not only to those who are easy to love but also those who are difficult to love. Sometimes hospitality may be showing agape love to someone who doesn't like your posts on social media, someone who does not think your grandkids are the cutest creatures God ever made, someone who votes differently from how you do, someone who has nothing to give in return.

How can we do that?

Read 1 John 4:7-8 in the margin. What is the source of love?

⁷Dear friends, let us love one another, for love comes from God. Everyone who loves has been born of God and knows God. ⁸Whoever does not love does not know God, because God is love.

(1 John 4:7-8)

These verses tell us that not only is God the source of love; God is love. Only through God's Spirit living in us can we hope to love others and be a part of koinonia, opening our lives to all—even those who stand against us (see 1 John 4:11-13).

Koinonia is not only for people with whom we agree but also people who need grace from us. And people from whom we need grace.

Where and with whom do you feel most safe? Most loved?

Is there a young mom, widow, or neighbor who could use some agape love from you? What can you do to express this love?

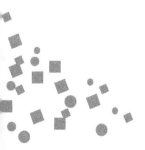

The word *hospital* is a Latin word to describe an apartment for guests and strangers.[3] In the first-century church, a *hospitalia* was a place where people were welcomed and cared for—more about connection than medicine. Many hospitals were created in remote and dangerous places to provide shelter for travelers.

If we are going to live in koinonia with others, we will be a "safe place" for those who are hurting, even those with whom we do not agree. When we offer kindness and safety to others, we communicate value to them—the same value we have to our God.

Call to Action

- Ask your pastor or women's ministry/Bible study leader if there is someone in the church who needs some hospitality in Jesus's name. Keep it simple and make a new friend.
- Are you aware of a missionary family who could use some encouragement? Call or send a card or package to encourage them. Be hospitable, even if they are halfway around the world. Encourage others to do the same.
- Sign up to bring a meal for a new foster family, a community member who just returned home from the hospital, missionaries on furlough, or a recent widow, or several of these, and take hospitality to them.
- Find a way to show hospitality to someone who is difficult to love. It might be as simple as being kind in response to unkind words or actions, offering a pleasant greeting when you see the person, or sending him or her an encouraging note.

Day 5: Some Light on the Subject of Hospitality

Today's "One Another"

But if we walk in the light, as he is in the light, we have fellowship with one another, and the blood of Jesus, his Son, purifies us from all sin.

(1 John 1:7)

Scripture Focus

Romans 12:13;
1 John 1:3-7

Hospitality is such a value to biblical community that it is listed as one of the virtues of elders (church leaders) in Titus 1:8. I so admire people who have the gift of hospitality. I also admire people who like to clean out their refrigerators, but that's another story!

In Romans 12:13, we are told to "share with the Lord's people who are in need. Practice hospitality." I am glad that Paul used the word *practice* when it comes to hospitality, because I am still practicing. There are people in my life who find great joy and fulfillment in opening their homes, hands, and tables to people, no matter the hour. Although I love when people come to visit and to break bread with us, I need advance notice—and that is not hospitality in its purest form; it is the desire to impress others.

I used to believe that hospitality was limited to opening one's home to others, but I have come to realize that, indeed, this is only a fraction of hospitality. Hospitality can be defined as serving others with love without complaint, taking on the expense and tasks with joy.

We used to have an elderly woman in our church who, when asked to bring a meal to a family, would go to her favorite local restaurant and order a meal. When she delivered the meal, she wanted to be able to fully concentrate on the family and not on the preparation; in doing so, she showed hospitality even though the meal was not in her home.

The apostle Paul benefited greatly from the hospitality of others. Anytime he mentions in his letters, also called epistles, those who extended kindness to him, he not only thanks them for opening their homes and hearts him but also encourages others to do likewise. Paul also extended a kind of hospitality to others. Just like the elderly woman in our church, he did not open his home but, instead, opened the opportunity for others to hear the gospel, whether Jew or Gentile, slave or free. He was intentional with the time that he spent with people, encouraging them in their pursuit of Jesus and loving them even at great personal sacrifice. Although for the most part Paul was nomadic (he did not have a permanent home), he chose to leave the comfort of a stable home and become a traveling missionary. Not limited to a certain location, he challenged Christians everywhere he went to live in biblical community. He invited throngs of people to join God's family, and his letters continue to invite people into a relationship with Jesus today.

What did hospitality look like in your home when you were growing up?

What stops you from being hospitable? What barriers to connection with others challenge you?

Perhaps you listed some logistical barriers, or perhaps some of your barriers have to do with your selfishness, pride, or some other sinful attitude. Or maybe there are sins of your past that have created barriers of darkness, making you feel unworthy of community or incapable of risking vulnerability and intimacy with others.

My family just bought new lighting fixtures for our dining room. When we bought the house, the lighting in the dining room was so dim that we could barely see our food in front of us at night. We saved up and found lighting that not only is decorative but also illuminates the whole room. We actually know what we are eating when it is in front of us! Light is so important for vision, clarity, and perspective. Our verse of the day provides such encouragement! "But if we walk in the light, as he is in the light, we have fellowship with one another, and the blood of Jesus, his Son, purifies us from all sin" (1 John 1:7). We are given a choice each day to turn from the darkness of our own guilt and shame, confess our sins, and walk in freedom—with others, with God, and with ourselves.

I am convinced that many of us become burdened by our past choices and choose to live in the darkness of regret instead of accepting forgiveness from Jesus and gaining encouragement from the fellowship found in Christ. We often choose to focus on the darkness of our choices instead of choosing to "walk in the light, as He is in the light." Our choices have consequences, and I think is it important to recognize the gravity of those choices; but when we remember that we can be purified by the blood of Jesus when we confess our trespasses, it seems foolish to walk in darkness anymore.

Read these verses, and then follow the instructions below:

³We proclaim to you what we have seen and heard, so that you also may have fellowship with us. And our fellowship is with the Father and with his Son, Jesus Christ. ⁴We write this to make our joy complete.

⁵This is the message we have heard from him and declare to you: God is light; in him there is no darkness at all. ⁶If we claim to have fellowship with him and yet walk in the darkness, we lie and do not live out the truth. ⁷But if we walk in the light, as he is in the light, we have fellowship with one another, and the blood of Jesus, his Son, purifies us from all sin.

(1 John 1:3-7)

1. **Draw a line under the phrases that pertain to us (us/we).**

2. **Draw two lines under the phrases that pertain to either God or His Son, or both.**

3. **Circle the words or phrases that pertain to light.**

4. **Draw a star above the words that pertain to fellowship or community.**

These verses imply that fellowship or connection with God produces fellowship with others. John uses the same word for "fellowship" in verses 3 and 6, which means that our fellowship or connection with God is in direct proportion to the quality or level of health we have with one another.

If we are going to truly embark on the Belonging Project, we must embrace the idea that we *need* fellowship with other believers—thus the

"If we . . ." language in verse 7. According to this verse, it is spiritually impossible to be out of fellowship or communion with one another while having complete connection or fellowship with God. Let that sink in a minute. Our loving connection to God determines our loving connection with others!

In their book *Experiencing God Together: God's Plan to Touch Your World*, Henry T. and Melvin D. Blackaby write,

> Evidence that we truly have fellowship with God is demonstrated by our fellowship with one another. If we are not experiencing true *koinonia* with God's people—or any one of God's people—we are not having *koinonia* with God or walking in the light as He is in the light. It is impossible to have a relationship with God and not share it with the rest of God's people. The deeper the relationship with God, the deeper the relationship becomes to God's people. The two are eminently connected.[4]

If I were to examine my spiritual life, the greatest seasons of growth and connection to God are in direct proportion to the connection I had with other people in my life. It was the mentoring I received, the caring I extended to others, and the time I spent connected to God's Word that were commonalities each time.

What does your fellowship with others reveal about your fellowship with God?

Is there anything you have done that is blocking your relationship with God and others? If so, confess it to God, receive His forgiveness, and offer forgiveness to yourself. Write a prayer of confession, or thanksgiving, or both, below.

Call to Action

- Hospitality is not limited to opening one's door or home to others; it includes connecting with others and with God. In fact, that connection is interrelated. What can you do to strengthen your connection with God? Make a plan and see how it affects your relationships with others also.
- I burn a candle at my house when guests are coming. I want my house to smell welcoming (actually, I want it to smell like I can bake cookies without burning them!). I want each person to feel valued and special in my home. What is a simple way you can make others feel valued and special in your home? Try something new this week.
- More important than any meal we might serve is offering people a safe place to be themselves and feel seen, heard, and loved. How can you offer "safe space" to someone this week?
- If we are to thrive in biblical community, we must learn how to open our homes and hearts (and candles!) to others and, in turn, honor God. It means leveraging the things God has given us to bring others closer to Him. Identify something God has given to you that you can leverage to bring others closer to Him.
- It may be fun to "spill the tea," hear "the juice," and talk about people, but that is not true loving connection or friendship and it is not honoring to God. In fact, it is destructive to the body of Christ and reflects poorly on everyone who participates. If someone has shared information with us, it is our job to protect that information and be a safe harbor for that person. Remember that gossip undermines hospitality and biblical community, so be a safe person who keeps confidences. Be extra sensitive this week to detect when catching up becomes gossip, and redirect the conversation.

Weekly Wrap-up

When kids are little, they often make best friends with others after playing for only two minutes in the park. A child may not even know the

other child's name, but they are suddenly best friends. As adults, we know that although that may seem adorable with kids, it is not realistic, nor is it deep connection.

Real fellowship and loving connection through the lens of biblical community is fostered by not slandering (or judging) one another, not grumbling against one another, practicing hospitality toward one another, and being humble with one another. It means working in the best interests of others and being a safe place for them.

I continue to hear from women all over the country just how lonely they are. As I travel the country speaking, I recognize that no matter the geography, the socioeconomic status, the denomination, or the educational background, loneliness seems to be universal. Disconnection is rampant, but God has better plans for each of us.

Connection and hospitality are so valuable to biblical community that they are listed as the duties of elders (church leaders) in Titus 1:8.

Fellowship and hospitality are directly connected. Practicing hospitality is the responsibility of all believers, yet we often shirk the responsibility, excusing ourselves by saying it is not our gift. We can all open our homes, apartments, condos, or front yards to others. We can also meet someone for coffee, bring a meal to his or her home, or just make some time at a local park for a quick prayer time. Hospitality can include all of those things, but it also can simply mean being a safe place for a struggling friend. Allowing God to use you through the discipline of active listening, keeping a secret, praying for the person, and choosing not to gossip can help you cultivate true fellowship through the practice of hospitality.

In doing so, we connect better with God and with others. The by-products often include a growing faith, dissipating loneliness, and satisfying relationships.

Fellowship with One Another

Deeper Connection Through the Lens of Biblical Community

We can connect more deeply with God and others by following Jesus's lead in loving and serving one another.

Welcome/Prayer/Icebreaker (5–10 minutes)

Welcome to Session 2 of *The Belonging Project: Finding Your Tribe and Learning to Thrive*. This week we've considered what real fellowship and loving connection look like through the lens of biblical community. Today we're exploring what it looks like to follow Jesus's lead and put aside our pride and judgment in order to love others well. We'll also look at how we can open our lives and our hearts (and maybe even our homes!) to others in order to form deeper connections.

Take a moment to open with prayer, and then go around the circle and share about a time when you felt completely at home and safe in someone else's space. What about his or her hospitality made you feel welcome?

Video (about 20 minutes)

Play the video segment for Week 2, filling in the blanks as you watch and making notes about anything that resonates with you or that you want to be sure to remember.

—Video Notes—

Scripture Focus: *John 13:14*

L_____ His ways.

L_____ in to service.

L_____ the way.

Other Insights:

Group Discussion (20–25 minutes for a 60-minute session; 30–35 minutes for a 90-minute session)

Video Discussion

- What are some modern ways that we can lean into service and "wash others' feet"?
- What are some things that stop us from leaning in to fully love one another?
- Although fellowship with other believers can be complicated, being a part of it grows and strengthens us. When is a time you experienced this?

Workbook Discussion

- Read James 4:11 aloud. James reminds us that we are brothers and sisters in Christ and should act accordingly. How does this Scripture ask us to treat one another?
- Read Matthew 18:15-19. How do these verses instruct us to handle conflict? (page 57)
- Have you ever confronted someone about something she or he was doing that was wrong? Did you have a full picture of the situation when you did so? What happened? (page 59)
- Who is the most humble person you know? How does that person show his or her humility? How does this person's humility affect others? (page 63)
- How do we clothe ourselves with humility? Describe some things we can do. (page 64)
- Why do you think hospitality is important in the life of the Body? (page 67)
- Read 1 John 4:7-8. What is the source of love? (page 68) Can you think of some specific ways we can express that love to others?
- What stops you from being hospitable? What barriers to connection with others challenge you? (page 71)

Connection Point (10–15 minutes—90-minute session only)

Divide into groups of two to three and discuss the following:

- Is there anything you have done or are doing (such as being judgmental, withholding hospitality, holding on to pride) that is blocking your relationship with God and others? (page 73)
- How is God prompting you to think or live differently as a result of what you've heard or learned this week?

Closing Prayer (5 minutes)

Close the session by sharing personal prayer requests and praying together. If you like, invite the women to surround those who have shared requests and pray for them aloud. In addition to praying aloud for one another, close by asking God to help you embrace His plan for biblical community and for the grace to humble yourselves and follow Jesus's lead in loving and serving others.

Week 3

Forgive One Another

Forgiveness Through the Lens of Biblical Community

Memory Verse

Bear with each other and forgive one another if any of you has a grievance against someone. Forgive as the Lord forgave you.

(Colossians 3:13)

Day 1: Payback

Today's "One Another"

Bear with each other and forgive one another if any of you has a grievance against someone. Forgive as the Lord forgave you.

(Colossians 3:13)

I know that I don't like everyone and not everyone likes me, but for the most part, I do not feel like I harbor bitterness toward anyone—well, except for the person who created pantyhose. I truly hate that guy. But against everyone else, I don't harbor bitterness.

At least I thought so. But then, a few years ago, my husband and I embarked on a discipleship program within our church. We worked through a guided curriculum, meeting with another couple in our church who encouraged and challenged us along the way. My husband was meeting with a godly man in our church who was walking through each chapter with him, and I was doing the same with his amazing wife.

I loved the process until we got to the chapter about forgiveness, and then I didn't like the plan so much. During our weekly meeting, my mentor asked me to create a list of the people against whom I was harboring bitterness. The idea was not that I was to build a case against them; instead, I was to ask for their forgiveness for the bitterness I was harboring against each person.

I stared at the blank page for a long time. I knew there were things for which I could ask forgiveness from my sister, my husband, and with some other family members, but I also knew there was someone in my life whom I struggled to love. But I knew if I put his name on my list, my mentor would make me call him. Make me ask for his forgiveness. Make me humble myself. I did not want to do it. This gentleman and I did not "spur one another on toward love and good deeds," which is a hard thing for coworkers, but even worse when the person was my boss. In fact, some days I would come home from work sick with stress because of the conversations we'd had at work.

I work for a Christian organization, but having a shared faith does not always guarantee that people will get along. I made my boss crazy. And he made me mad. And I, frankly, was comfortable staying mad at him long after he left the organization. I did not want to call him. I did not want to give up my anger toward him because I felt my anger was justified. I didn't want to consider extending forgiveness to him.

So I left his name off of the list, thinking that it would get me off the hook. It didn't work. When this wonderful woman and I were sitting across the table from each other in a nearby café, she asked, "Since making the list, have you thought of anyone else you need to ask forgiveness from?" I could feel the muscles in my jaw tighten. "Anyone?" she asked. I took a long, slow breath. Then I spoke, my words accompanied by tears, anger, and justification. And then humiliation. I was embarrassed to tell this woman about my pettiness; I was struck by my complete disregard for realizing the forgiveness I've been given in Jesus and extending that same forgiveness to my boss.

That night, I picked up the phone. I prayed that he wouldn't answer the phone and when he did, I wanted to hang up. Stupid caller ID. If I did hang up, he would know it was me, and I was a little old for prank calling, so I mustered the strength and said, "Hey, can we talk?"

He was very kind. He and I shared very superficial conversation about family and new ministries and then it happened. I mustered up the courage and said, "I'm sorry." I apologized for the anger I held on to; I apologized for the times that I did not display grace and was self-righteous. I apologized for not being generous in my assumptions of him and then asked for his forgiveness. He forgave me and then asked for my forgiveness in return. There was nothing magical about our exchange, but I'm so thankful that I put his name on the list.

> **Are you are harboring a secret (or not-so-secret) bitterness against anyone in your life? From whom might you need to seek forgiveness?**

My hero when it comes to forgiving others is Joseph, whose beautiful and heartbreaking story is found in Genesis 37–50.

Here's what happened, in a nutshell. Joseph, the next-to-youngest of Jacob's sons, is favored by his father and therefore hated by his brothers. It didn't help that Joseph has visions and dreams that deepen the chasm between him and his jealous brothers and drive them crazy. One day his dad gives him a special, ornate coat that inspires a musical (okay, that part doesn't happen until the early 1970s). Fed up, Joseph's brothers sell him into slavery and tell their father he is dead. He ends up in the home of an influential Egyptian official, where he finds favor, but is then is wrongly accused, imprisoned, and forgotten then is forgiven, exalted to a powerful position in Egypt, and ultimately saves many people from famine. *Whew.*

Lots of *really* dramatic things happen in this story, but the most unbelievable part for me happens when Joseph's brothers come back into the picture many years later. At that time, Joseph is basically in charge of all of Egypt, and his brothers come to him for help, not knowing he is the same brother they had discarded all those years ago. Instead of pummeling them with anger and condemnation, Joseph confronts these brothers—who had robbed him of years with his father, the comforts of home, and decades of his life—and he forgives them.

> **Read Genesis 45:1-8. What emotions does Joseph display in this meeting? What about the brothers? What thoughts and feelings do you think were behind their emotions?**

> **Look up Genesis 50:20. Why does Joseph say he is able to forgive his brothers?**

In what areas of your life have you seen God redeem a hurt or injustice?

Even though it was written thousands of years after Joseph's story, Today's "One Another" verse is such a reflection of Joseph's attitude. The apostle Paul, writing to the church at Colossae, says: "Bear with each other and forgive one another if any of you has a grievance against someone. Forgive as the Lord forgave you" (Colossians 3:13).

Biblical community is not for sissies. We are a broken people, and even when made holy by the blood of Jesus, we sometimes make "broken" choices. We speak unkindly, we act unfairly, we give grace unequally. Community with other believers can be challenging and can take a lot of faith, but it is a gift and it is worth the hard work of extending and embracing forgiveness.

Righteousness and justice are the foundation of your throne; love and faithfulness go before you. (Psalm 89:14)

Sometimes, it is people in the church who wrong us. Even church leaders are not immune from hurting others, and many of us have scars from hurtful exchanges in the church. It's important to note that forgiving someone does not mean overlooking wrongs that have been committed or giving a pass to the offender so that he or she bypasses the consequences of those actions.

Learn to do right; seek justice. Defend the oppressed. Take up the cause of the fatherless; plead the case of the widow. (Isaiah 1:17)

Read the verses in the margin and answer the following questions:

What does Psalm 89:14 tell us about God?

How does Isaiah 1:17 encourage us to seek justice?

According to Micah 6:8, what does the Lord require of us?

He has shown you, O mortal, what is good. And what does the LORD require of you? To act justly and to love mercy and to walk humbly with your God.
(Micah 6:8)

Our God is a God of both justice and mercy, and He wants us to practice both as well. Though God promises to redeem bad situations and work all things for good for those who are called according to His purpose (Romans 8:28), sometimes consequences are a necessary part of bringing about that redemption.

Have you ever been reluctant to grant forgiveness because you thought it would excuse the wrong behavior? If so, describe the situation briefly:

How is it possible to forgive and seek justice simultaneously? Have you ever experienced or witnessed that? If so, write about it briefly:

Can you think of a time when the consequences of your own or others' actions have led to a redemptive outcome? If so, describe it briefly:

To truly grasp what it means to forgive others, we need to understand the phrase "Forgive as the Lord forgave you" (Colossians 3:13).

**Read Romans 5:8 in the margin. How did God demon-
strate His love for us?**

Romans 5:8 reminds us that we contributed *nothing* to the forgiveness
God showed each of us. He forgave us before we prayed a prayer, discov-
ered our need, sought His face, knew His name, or asked for forgiveness.
He always gives more than He gets.

That is the forgiveness He models for us. He puts the *give* in *forgiveness*.
We should do the same. If we are going to thrive in biblical community,
we must forgive one another and remove any barriers to true connection.

**In his Letter to the Colossians, Paul continues to instruct
the believers about how to live with one another. Read
Colossians 3:14-17. Below, make a brief list of what he
instructs the believers to do in each verse.**

Verse 14:

Verse 15:

Verse 16:

Verse 17:

Which of these instructions most resonates with you?

What is one way you can implement Paul's instructions in your own community of believers?

Though we will never be able to forgive others as fully as God forgives us, nevertheless He does call us to live in harmony with one another, and forgiveness is a tool that can make that happen. When God calls us to forgive, He will give us the strength and the grace to do so. He will equip us as we draw on His power and love.

Forgiveness vs. Reconciliation

Forgiveness and reconciliation are not the same. It takes one to forgive, but it takes two to reconcile. Just as forgiveness does not mean we must excuse wrong behavior, forgiveness also does not require us to reconcile with the one who wronged us. Sometimes reconciliation is not possible (such as when the other person is deceased or unwilling), and sometimes it is not advisable (such as when reconciliation would put us or others in danger).

Call to Action

- Make a list of things from the past week for which you need to ask forgiveness from Jesus. Spend some time in prayer confessing these things and thanking Him for His forgiveness.
- Ask the Lord where you can grow in your ability to extend forgiveness to others. Where is He leading you to extend forgiveness to another? What next steps do you need to take?

Day 2: Grace Space

Today's "One Another"

"Therefore confess your sins to each other and pray for each other so that you may be healed. The prayer of a righteous person is powerful and effective."

(James 5:16)

I used to take my kids to this little pizza place in the middle of town that was basically a Chuck E. Cheese knockoff. Of course, my kids loved it. The management played VeggieTales videos on perpetual loop, served terribly mediocre pizza, and had an arcade and a large prize "store" with a thousand cheap toys, games, and gadgets available. Among the prizes that the kids could win with their tickets was a large array of sticky hands. I hate sticky hands.

If you are unaware of the travesty of sticky hands, let me educate you. Sticky hands are a gelatinous hand-shaped toy with a "tail" that you can grab and then chuck the sticky hand toward something with the intention of having it stick. My kids would spend hours throwing that little sticky hand onto walls, refrigerators, and anything else they thought it might stick to. In my eyes, it is the worst invention ever.

Because the hands are sticky, they pick up any residue or dust on the surface where they are attached. So after an hour of playing, as if my kids didn't have enough germs, the sticky hand would have picked up all the germs from every surface in their play area. It was a literal "prom" of germs!

Eventually the sticky hands would lose some of their "stick" and would slide down the wall and get stuck on the carpet. And that nasal mucus–textured hand would transform into hairy Chewbacca snot. Disgusting—and my kids couldn't get enough of it!

One afternoon while at this sticky hands mecca restaurant, I gave each of my kids a certain number of tokens and allowed them to play any of the arcade games. They knew they needed a certain number of tickets to earn sticky hands for themselves, and they had their eyes on the prize. I just wanted to sit at a table and read a book, and I knew this would buy me a little bit of time. However, after only a few minutes, my

daughter came to the table where I was sitting and held up two tokens. She needed help earning tickets, and she knew just the person for the job: me. See, while some of you have the gift of hospitality, or of giving, or of administration, I have the spiritual gift of Skee-Ball. Yes. Skee-Ball. And by the way, it is not bragging if it is true, so I am not bragging, but I am really good at Skee-Ball. While most people get two or three tickets for each token, it is not unlike me to get ten or fifteen tickets a round playing Skee-Ball. My daughter was short of tickets and so she placed the tokens in my hands; her future was squarely on my shoulders.

Her confidence in me was not unfounded. With the first token, I earned fifteen tickets. Lights on the Skee-Ball machine were flashing and the beeps on the machine were getting louder, all signals that indeed, I had done a great job. Fifteen tickets earned. However, when the tickets began to dispense, more than fifteen tickets came out. More than thirty. More than a hundred. In fact, the entirety of the ticket roll emptied onto the floor.

My daughter was elated. She began dancing and singing around the arcade and grabbing the attention of all within a twenty-mile radius. She was excited—so excited, in fact, she told her brother that between the two of them, they could get at least three sticky hands apiece with the tickets I had just gleaned.

But I told her that they were not our tickets. I explained that I'd only earned fifteen tickets, and we needed to contact a worker to straighten things out. A moment or so later, a very unenthusiastic employee arrived. He explained that indeed the machine had malfunctioned, but since it was in my favor, I would be able to keep all the tickets. My kids began a song-and-dance celebration in the middle of that arcade. The praise-and-worship session that they began had everything except the offering plate. They were grateful to God for His bounty and they let Him know it.

Just then a very young child pulled on the hem of my shirt. "Excuse me. Can I have some tickets?"

I leaned down to get on an eye level with this young lady. "Of course you can, sweetheart." I turned to see my son and daughter with the deer in headlights look. "She can have some tickets, right?" They shook their heads in unison. My son broke the silence. "No. These are *our* tickets."

I spoke through my gritted teeth, "We will give this girl some tickets. And we will smile and be gracious about it, won't we?" The worship service was over. My kids were in full King Midas mode. My daughter was the first to speak. "Fine," she said. "You can have two tickets."

My face grew flushed with anger. "May I remind you that we deserved fifteen tickets and we got at least twenty times that."

She finally acquiesced. "OK," she said again. "You can have three tickets."

The three-point sermon that ensued once we got back in our minivan was louder and with more conviction than I'd ever preached. I was really disappointed in my kids. And then it hit me: don't we often do the same thing when it comes to extending grace toward other people?

Scripture is clear: God does not treat us as our sins deserve (Psalm 103:10). Instead, we are given grace. And yet, with other people, we begrudgingly give them three tickets' worth of grace instead of sharing the overflowing bounty of grace that God has given us. We focus on what we deserve because we work hard or because we go to Bible study or because we said no to a cookie. We rarely focus on the fact that we deserved condemnation and instead we were given love. We deserved death and we were given life.

Author and speaker Louie Giglio says it this way: "Why are we spooning out mercy when God gives it to us in shovel-fuls?"[1]

Can you recall a time when you wanted to spoon out mercy rather than give it in shovelfuls? If so, why were you reluctant to offer grace?

How did your refusal of grace affect the other party? How did it affect you?

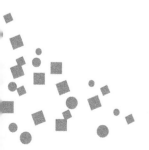

When Jesus walked on earth, he chose twelve men to walk alongside Him in His years of ministry. Despite the fact that these men saw Him defy physics by walking on water, have dominion over demons, heal the sick, give sight to the blind, calm the storm, and feed thousands in one sitting, they still could not stop bickering.

If they could not maintain harmony in their ranks—while literally standing right next to Jesus—what makes us think we are any different? If they could not avoid jealousy, bragging, and disunity, why should we think we can avoid challenges when it comes to biblical community? We human beings are obviously predisposed to selfishness and self-protection, but Jesus shows us a better way.

> **Look up John 13:34-35. In your own words, write what happens in those verses:**

> **Read John 13:1-12. What does Jesus do for his disciples? Why does He say He was doing it (v. 15)?**

> **Can you recall a time that you lavishly served someone, perhaps even someone who didn't deserve it? What prompted you to act as you did?**

> **How do you think you'd react if Jesus asked to wash your feet? How might you respond?**

What command does Jesus give the disciples in verses 34-35?

James, the brother of Jesus, was there that night Jesus washed the disciples' feet, and he heard Jesus speak a vision for His followers that night.

Years later, he penned the Book of James. (Although there are numerous references to a man named James in the Bible, most biblical scholars agree that the Book of James was written by James, Jesus's brother.) By the time the book was written, much had changed. Jesus had died and was resurrected, some of the apostles had been persecuted, the church was growing, and there was some conflict in the new churches. Just like today, there were interpersonal relationships within the early church that were tumultuous and divisive. This may have been the catalyst for why James wrote the words in Today's "One Another" verse.

Therefore confess your sins to each other and pray for each other so that you may be healed. The prayer of a righteous person is powerful and effective.
(James 5:16)

Read James 5:16 in the margin. According to this verse, what happens when we confess our sins and pray for one another?

How does this verse's command work in tandem with Jesus's command in John 13:34-35?

Jesus wanted us to know that holding on to unforgiveness is clearly unhealthy for us, and today we can back up that wisdom with scientific research. According to Johns Hopkins Medicine, it can be a true hazard: "Whether it's a simple spat with your spouse or long-held resentment toward a family member or friend, unresolved conflict can go deeper than you may realize—it may be affecting your physical health. The good news: Studies have found that the act of forgiveness can reap huge rewards for your health, lowering the risk of heart attack; improving cholesterol levels and sleep; and reducing pain, blood pressure, and levels of anxiety, depression and stress. And research points to an increase in the forgiveness-health connection as you age."[2]

It is hard to hold on to bitterness when you pray for someone and confess your bitterness and anger. It's even kind of miraculous. When we lift people in prayer to God with honesty and sincerity, the Holy Spirit softens our hearts and releases us from the burden of unforgiveness. Confessing one's sins leaves one vulnerable and is difficult work, but such rawness not only reconnects us with our sister or brother in Christ, it deepens our own connection to God.

> **What most appeals to you about living and sharing life with other believers? What challenges have you faced in living in this way?**

> **In what ways have you witnessed the Lord growing you through biblical community?**

If we convince ourselves that living in biblical community will be simple and without complications, we will be disappointed and, eventually, disillusioned. However, if we embrace the difficulties of biblical community and still choose it, we can grow in our Christlikeness.

Call to Action

- Pray for healing in your church and community. Ask God to show you new ways to love one another and set an example for others.
- Gather with a group of other believers. Pray that God would show you how to best love those around you. You might want to take Communion together or wash one another's feet. You might want to exchange names and commit to pray for one another this week. You might want to join together to serve in some way. Ask the Lord to guide you into deeper community as you spend time together.

Day 3: Jean Pool

Scripture Focus

Philippians 2:5-8

Today's "One Another"

Live in harmony with one another. Do not be proud, but be willing to associate with people of low position. Do not be conceited.

(Romans 12:16)

The year I turned eleven, there was only one item on my Christmas list: a pair of designer jeans I wanted more than oxygen. My denim dream had a small swan on one of the pockets and the attention of every preteen in my life. Such a pair would cost my parents more then they would normally spend on Christmas gifts, but that year, my mom took part of her clothing budget and purchased those beauties for me.

They fit like a glove. They fit like they were made for me and only me—well, for a few months at least. The problem was, I ate food somewhere between that beautiful Christmas morning and the summer trip to Girl Scout camp.

Because of my age, that year my mother decided it was past time for me to pack my own suitcase as I got ready for camp. However, when I put those jeans in my suitcase, my mother raised an eyebrow. "Sweetheart, are you sure you want to take those? They are a bit tight." By "a bit tight," she meant that they were *really* tight. So tight that I had to suck

in my spleen in order to put them on in the mornings. But they were my favorite jeans in the whole world and so I packed them, much to my mother's chagrin.

I did not wear my Gloria Vanderbilt jeans until the second day of camp. That day my Girl Scout leader decided it was time to play hide-and-seek. Looking back, she was probably already tired of a dozen or so giggling eleven- and twelve-year-old girls, but it sounded like fun to us. Well, it sounded like fun to my peers in my troop. I, on the other hand, was almost a foot taller than most of the girls and a bit heavier than most. I could never contort my body to fit in small spaces like my class-mates could, so hide-and-seek was never much fun for me.

The leader started to count down, and I headed for the tallest, largest tree. I not only had my stature to hide but also my giant eighties hair (I wish you could have seen it; it was glorious). I ventured quite a ways when I finally found the perfect tree. Its trunk was so thick that I could easily hide up in the tree without fear of being spotted. It was a good spot...so good that I stayed there for what seemed like an eternity; I only heard the voice of my leader a couple of times. I grew bored. I grew weary. I started to slide slowly down the trunk to climb down. That was a huge mistake.

It was not the sound of ripping material that was my first clue; I heard nothing. It was the breeze. I could actually feel a cool breeze. Not on my arms, mind you, but on my backside, through my Fruit of the Looms. My glorious Gloria Vanderbilt jeans had ripped from the loops in the back to the zipper compartment in the front. I was mortified. Not just because of the ripped jeans, because I knew it would mean the mockery of my troop mates.

I could hear my troop leader. She began to call my name, and soon the tone of her voice became more serious. I did not want to be found. The last time she called my name, I could hear a little bit of panic in her voice. I stretched out my right arm so that she could see it from behind the tree. I could hear her pace quicken and the sound of her steps come closer.

"Are you OK? Are you hurt?" she asked.

I shook my head. "No," I answered, "but I am not standing up."

"What's wrong?" She asked.

I replied with the only answer I could muster, "I am not standing up."

After I saw the puzzled look on her face mix with concern, I spilled the beans. I explained that I ripped my pants, but was unsure of the extent of the damage. I lied. I knew. I knew it was huge. She assured me that it probably was not that big of a deal. And then I stood up. And she recognized that indeed, it was a big deal. That is when the tears began. Tears of embarrassment. Tears of fear. Tears of loss. I felt her arm on my shoulder.

"It's OK," she said. "I have an idea." She untied the cardigan sweater around her middle and wrapped it around mine. She explained that when we returned to camp, I was to say nothing. She would distract the girls while I made my way to the cabin to change clothes. No one else needed to know, she said. It would be our little secret.

It was just a cardigan sweater, but it meant so much more to me. It meant that I had a confidant. It meant that somebody was on my team. I never forgot it.

In a church, such exchanges are more rare than I would like. Sometimes, in the Christian community, we witness great men and women of God who make terrible choices, then watch other men and women of God take pleasure in pointing out all the flaws, all the sins, all the drama that unfolds.

If we are to fulfill the verse of the day and live in harmony with one another, we must leave our pride aside and associate with people who have made terrible choices—and love them enough to make sure they don't stay in that mess.

We need to follow the example of Jesus when it comes to humility. His sacrifice covered our sin and shame forever. In a sense, He wrapped a cardigan sweater of grace over our pain and devastation and told us it would be all right. And then He died on the cross to make sure it would be.

How do you define *humility*?

Read Philippians 2:5-8 in the margin. How did Jesus's life display humility?

Do you consider humility one of your strengths or weaknesses? Why? In what area do you most struggle with pride?

Today's verse, Romans 12:16, is so practical: "Live in harmony with one another. Do not be proud, but be willing to associate with people of low position. Do not be conceited." Let's break the verse down a little and explore how we can embrace humility in loving and forgiving others.

The verse begins with : "Live in harmony with one another." Immediately this makes me think of music.

I love singing on my church's worship team. I do not have a terrific voice, but I am really proficient at singing harmony—the notes in the chord above or below the melody line that accentuate and enhance the melody. If we are to live in harmony with one another, we have to cast aside being the center of attention or being the boss. We consider our place as one member of the body of Christ, and work to make others feel supported and loved; we accentuate the strengths of others.

Read Romans 12:3-8. What does this verse tell us about how to live with one another in harmony?

The verse continues, "Do not be proud, but be willing to associate with people of low position."

5-8Think of yourselves the way Christ Jesus thought of himself. He had equal status with God but didn't think so much of himself that he had to cling to the advantages of that status no matter what. Not at all. When the time came, he set aside the privileges of deity and took on the status of a slave, became human! Having become human, he stayed human. It was an incredibly humbling process. He didn't claim special privileges. Instead, he lived a selfless, obedient life and then died a selfless, obedient death—and the worst kind of death at that— a crucifixion.
(Philippians 2:5-8 MSG)

Frankly, this part is easier for me to consider. You see, I never sat at the popular table in high school. I never was prom queen or homecoming royalty. I was just me. I wore pink leopard-print pants and was both a drama geek and a cheerleader. I was in the Spanish Honor Society and the Student Council, but I never blinked at associating with any of the other kids in my class.

But, as an adult, this gets trickier. For example, how should I react when someone makes bad choices and is disgraced in the eyes of my community? What do I say to the person drowning in shame over the disaster he or she has caused? I have to set aside any self-righteousness if biblical community with that person is going to thrive.

> **What does Jesus say in Matthew 9:10-17 about how to treat others who might be considered "of low position"? What about this verse resonates with you the most?**

> **Have you ever reached out to someone who was discarded or condemned by your community? How did he or she react, and what happened as a result? If not, is there anyone you might need reach out to today?**

Today's verse ends with, "Do not be conceited."

I have always thought of conceit as an unhealthy, unbalanced love of oneself. I think of pride as a cousin of conceit: unhealthy, unbalanced overestimation of one's importance.

Again, I am still at the nerd table. And I think conceit is not a problem for me, but pride sure is. It seems to creep up at the most inopportune times—like, oh, *always*.

Sometimes people hurt my feelings, or say mean things on social media, or disappoint me. But when I let my hurt feelings and pride sever connection with people or God, my conceit is an issue.

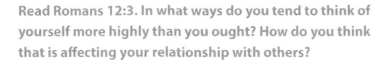

Read Romans 12:3. In what ways do you tend to think of yourself more highly than you ought? How do you think that is affecting your relationship with others?

Romans 3:23-24 tells us why harmony among believers will never be perfect. What are the challenges for biblical community, and what is our hope?

What might "live in harmony with one another" look like in your life?

We, the body of Christ, are a choir of sorts. We all have different parts to fill, we have a Conductor, and we are called to work together. And when there are choir members who are not stars, who can barely hold their notes, we are called to associate with them and help—and that means we also allow people to help us when we are the ones struggling. We remember that we have a responsibility to work in the best interest of the choir. Harmony in the church is never perfect, but it can be beautiful.

Call to Action

- Pray for those in your community whose views and positions are different from yours.
- Pray for politicians with whom you do not agree.

- Pray that God would show you how to live in harmony without watering down your convictions.
- As the Lord leads, reach out to someone in your community who has had a public failure or made mistakes and ask how you can encourage and support him or her.

Day 4: I Give It a Ten

Scripture Focus

John 17:20-23

Today's "One Another"

I appeal to you, brothers and sisters, in the name of our Lord Jesus Christ, that all of you agree with one another in what you say and that there be no divisions among you, but that you be perfectly united in mind and thought.

(I Corinthians 1:10)

I love to talk. I used to get in trouble for it in school all the time. (For the record, I often think those things that get us in trouble in class often make money as adults. Worked for me!) I used to talk so much, in fact, that teachers would isolate me. Even when our class got a Chinese exchange student who spoke no English whatsoever, I got him in trouble for talking!

My talking has gotten me into hot water for a couple of reasons: Sometimes, I share a story that is not mine to tell. Once in a while, I repeat a story I have heard without making sure it is true. There are other times that I jump in to tell a story without fully listening to the other person. Although I have learned from those mistakes, the toughest lesson for me was discerning with whom I can safely share secrets. I am overly trusting, you see.

Once, after a particularly rotten day in junior high (I had a lot of those), my mom sat me down to help me sort out the happenings of the day. That morning before school, I had shared a secret to a person I thought was a friend and then found out that she had blabbed my secret to everyone in the junior high by morning recess. Even after all these years, when recalling this story, I want to punch her in the throat (in Jesus's name, of course).

Have you ever have a falling out with a friend who mattered to you? Do you remember what the argument was about?

If you could go back and remedy the situation and fix the friendship (or another relational situation that might come to mind), would you? Why or why not? What would you do differently?

As a result of my humiliating junior high betrayal, my mom devised a rating system of sorts to help me determine who I should share my secrets with. For example, a "10" friend is someone who works in your best interest, roots for your rise, celebrates your successes, and loves you enough to bring to your attention the areas in which you need improvement (even if it is just pointing out when you have broccoli in your teeth). He or she will laugh and cry with you. In areas where your opinions are different, he or she will respect you, listen to your side, and will not get defensive in the process. Your secrets are safe and will never leave his or her mouth for anyone but Jesus in silent prayer.

A "7" friend is someone who is loads of fun to be with. He or she may laugh and cry with you, but is not safe with information other than "common knowledge" stuff. You can enjoy time together, but hard conversations are to be avoided because conflict is not handled in a healthy way.

A "3" friend may be a teammate, classmate, or peer at work. Although you have a shared interest or location, he or she is not safe with information because he or she is either too new in your life to know gory details or has proven to be untrustworthy.

There is nothing biblical about this rating system, but it was a great help to me as I navigated the tumultuous social waters of high school and college. I also recently taught it to my daughter, and just as I pray for myself, I pray that she would be a "10" friend to those God places in her path.

But can we—or should we—use such a system when attempting to thrive in our community of believers? In biblical community, just as in any scenario where humans are involved, there are people who disappoint and hurt others. Just because someone has Jesus in his or her heart does not mean that, once in biblical community, he or she is instantly a safe place or that you will agree on everything.

In order to learn how to handle disagreements in a biblical way, let's examine Today's "One Another" verse more. The church members at Corinth were struggling with disagreements, and so Paul wrote these words to instruct and guide them.

I appeal to you, brothers and sisters, in the name of our Lord Jesus Christ, that all of you agree with one another in what you say and that there be no divisions among you, but that you be perfectly united in mind and thought.
(1 Corinthians 1:10)

Let's look again at 1 Corinthians 1:10 in the margin. Paul begins with "I appeal to you, brothers and sisters, in the name of our Lord Jesus Christ." Why do you think he starts off this way?

What three things does Paul instruct these believers to do?

1.

2.

3.

What reaction do you have to Paul's words, considering them in the context of biblical community?

Um, OK, Paul. Yeah, right. I imagine these church members, engaged in bitter disputes with one another, think Paul might have gone off his rocker a little bit this time.

Paul understood the importance of unity among believers. He was a religious zealot who, before understanding the true identity of Jesus, spent much of his adult life trying to destroy the church. He appeals to the church in Corinth and reminds them of who they are in relationship to one another and reminds them in Whose name they are united. The very use of the name of Jesus reminds them of the grace they had all received and His call to work together for the hope of the gospel.[3]

What role should forgiveness play in our unity with other believers? How important do you think it is?

Although the apostle Paul no doubt knew that perfect unity is only possible in heaven, he also knew that schisms between believers send mixed messages to unbelievers looking in.

Today, with all the varied cultures, backgrounds, educational levels, and perspectives among modern-day believers, there is no way to agree with one another on every topic, but there is a way to ensure that no one is undermined by another believer—by agreeing on how the love of God is to be presented to those outside of the church. The words we use should be for a united purpose, with a united language, and with a united doctrine of Jesus as Lord.

Some churches use a unifying mission statement or recite the Apostles' Creed to focus the thoughts of the members of the congregation. Some churches unite with other congregations in their community (despite theological and cultural differences) to remind participants of commonalities.

> **Look up John 17:20-23. What is Jesus's prayer for those who believe in Him?**

> **Why do you think it so important for the body of Christ to be united?**

> **What can you do to foster unity in your church? your small group? your friendships?**

Unity does not mean we agree on everything, but as believers in Christ, we *must* be united on the idea that Jesus is the Son of God, that He died on the cross and rose on the third day, that He lived a sinless life and conquered sin and death.

In addition, we must act accordingly. We must love accordingly. We need to be "10" friends for the biblical community in our life and support one another, even when our opinions differ. We must find the common ground of Jesus; He is enough to unite us.

Call to Action

- When you are confronted by another believer's point of view that is different from your own, suppress the desire to react immediately, and stop and ask God to guide you in your interactions with that person. Prayerfully consider: is your point of view something that perhaps needs to be reconsidered, based on Scripture?

- For the next day or so, with every interaction you have with another person, whether he or she is a believer or not, work hard to establish something on which you can both agree. Practice unity, it is a major part of commUNITY.

Day 5: Berry Nice

Today's "One Another"

Be kind and compassionate to one another, forgiving each other, just as in Christ God forgave you.

(Ephesians 4:32)

Scripture Focus

Lamentations 3:22-23; Hebrews 12:14-15

When my husband and I lived in Southern California, our apartment was near a seasonal strawberry stand. The stand was located in the fields where these beautiful, fragrant, huge, delicious strawberries were picked. We knew that the stand would open soon when we could smell the scent of berry sweetness wafting through our neighborhood. The stand was close enough that we often would walk there, so we would often start our Saturdays by strolling to the stand and then going off to run errands. We spent many a Saturday night sick from overeating the strawberries we had gleaned in the morning. We would eat so many that the roofs of our mouths would be tender and raw, but we didn't care. They were worth it.

One particular morning, my husband woke me up early. Now, let me point out that when we went to premarital counseling, the counselor covered all of the areas he thought were important: intimacy, family, good communication, and so forth, but he missed something. He missed covering the challenges included if one spouse was a morning person and the other one is a night person. You see, I am totally a night owl. Left to my own devices, I will read until all hours of the morning, but getting up early isn't my speed. My husband, on the other hand, is downright pleasant in the morning. He's a delight. He's cheerful. It's incredibly frustrating.

So he woke me early that morning, but even my grumpiness could not stop me from my quest for strawberries. I sleepily looked around the room for something to wear, and that is when I spotted the jeans I had worn the night before. I had worn them for only a couple of hours, I told myself, so they couldn't be all that dirty. I threw them on, found a comfy T-shirt, wrangled my curly hair into a ponytail, and headed out. After we picked up the strawberries, we turned for home. Just about the time we got to the apartment, my husband suggested that we hit the road and tackle our to-do list. My husband is actually really fun to shop with, so I gladly obliged; however, I prayed I wouldn't see anybody I knew.

If you ever have any doubt that prayer works, pray a prayer like that. Pray a prayer that you won't see anybody you know. Because that's when God shows the depth of His glorious sense of humor. If you pray not to see anyone, he will send your entire ZIP code of friends, families, long-distance relatives, ex-boyfriends, and current bosses to your exact location. And that's what happened. I saw a zillion people I knew.

When we got into the third store, I saw a really cute shirt and decided to try it on, so I got into the dressing room, pulled the shirt over my head, and turned around to see what it looked like from the back. I nearly screeched at what I saw, which was a huge lump on my backside. I was born with only two buns, but that day it clearly looked as though I had a third one. I reached inside my jeans and discovered my underwear from the night before balled up and stuck inside my pants.

I'm confident that I made the church prayer list that day. I imagine all the cute older ladies in my church saying, "Please pray for Amberly. She has a third bun." I felt like an idiot. And I didn't end up buying the T-shirt.

What is an embarrassing moment you can recall? Was it the result of something you did, or was someone else the cause of it?

How do you tend to handle embarrassing situations? What messages tend to play in your head when those kinds of things happen?

This week we have been discussing forgiveness in biblical community, and I believe we would be remiss if we didn't remind ourselves that we need to extend God's forgiveness to ourselves as well. I know I certainly need that reminder.

I do not have the market cornered on doing stupid things, but I certainly have done my fair share. For example, I am a talker, not a great listener, so sometimes, in the spirit of making conversation, I put my size-eleven feet squarely in my mouth and say exactly the wrong thing. And no, the bottom of my shoes do not taste delicious.

You may not, like me, say totally inappropriate things to others, but have you ever really paid attention to the things you think as you look in the mirror? If I said to a stranger on the street, "My gosh, girl, you *gotta* cut back on the bread," I would deserve the slap I would certainly receive. If I said to a friend, "You are not enough. No one is fooled. You're a real disappointment," I wouldn't have that friend for long, and rightly so.

And yet I say those things to myself all the time. I let my poor choices from the past find me and I relive those embarrassments and disappointments over and over and beat myself up again and again. And just like those undies in my jeans, it begins to disfigure me spiritually.

Do you have a hard time forgiving yourself? What is the most prevalent message you tell yourself when no one is around?

Think through some of your greatest regrets. Have you asked Jesus for forgiveness for those things? Have you forgiven yourself for those things?

Read Lamentations 3:22-23. What does this verse say to you about how the Lord sees our mistakes?

Forgiving ourselves is hard. I am imperfect. I make mistakes. But once I ask God for forgiveness, I need to forgive myself. I need to walk in freedom from my own condemnation.

But when I continue to beat myself up, my lack of forgiveness flows over into my life into other areas of my being, and eventually it spills over into how I deal with other people.

In fact, it usually happens that the very areas in which I have trouble in my own life—my sin patterns, old habits, and poor choices—are the very areas that I am shortest in forgiveness when it comes to other people.

Do you know the type of people with whom I am most impatient? Impatient people!

Which qualities of other people tend to annoy you the most? Why do you think this is the case?

Read Hebrews 12:14-15 in the margin. What stands out to you in this passage?

Have you ever witnessed roots of bitterness corrupt a relationship? What happened, and what might have prevented that root from spreading?

When I was growing up, my sister and I grew tired of the pat answer my parents always gave when we argued. They would always say, "Practice being nice." U*gh*. We laugh about it today, but at the time it was fodder for therapy.

Now a parent myself, I know why they said it. Because when we practice doing things, over time they become easier and develop into habits. Now, I find it easy to be nice to my sister because I spent time practicing that kindness.

In Today's "One Another" verse, Ephesians 4:32, Paul reminds the church in Ephesus to "be kind and compassionate to one another" and to "[forgive] each other" in order to develop habits of holiness and to remember just how much God has forgiven them.

What is one way today you can practice being kind and compassionate to yourself? To others?

Myself

[14]Work at living in peace with everyone, and work at living a holy life, for those who are not holy will not see the Lord. [15]Look after each other so that none of you fails to receive the grace of God. Watch out that no poisonous root of bitterness grows up to trouble you, corrupting many.
(Hebrews 12:14-15 NLT)

Others

What is one way you can extend forgiveness to your-self? What is one way you can extend forgiveness to another?

Myself

Others

Forgiving ourselves may be the hardest lesson of this study for some of us. Beating ourselves up for mistakes we have made, words we have misspoken, and patterns of poor choices is easy. Releasing the guilt of those choices, asking for forgiveness from God, and then accepting that forgiveness is another thing altogether. But it is a necessary step in healthy, biblical community.

Call to Action

- When you're tempted to bash yourself over a mistake, remember that God's mercies are new every day (Lamentations 3:22-23). Ask the Lord to forgive you and then help you to move on.

- Meditate on Psalm 139, and write down what God says about how He made you.
- Continue to work on extending forgiveness to someone who may have wronged you. Pray about what next steps you need to take, and ask God to guide and strengthen you as you act.

Weekly Wrap-up

The story of the prodigal son is such a powerful one. The wayward son, who returns after getting tired of hunger, fatigue, and the smell of pig slop, comes home to the open arms of his father. The father welcomes him home with forgiveness and a barbecue (Luke 15:11-32).

Nothing says forgiveness like a barbecue. I am a Texan at heart. I know these things!

As believers in Jesus, we need to never forget that our heavenly Father forgave us when we were wayward, ran toward us when He recognized our need, and threw a feast to celebrate our homecoming.

We need always to remember the stench of pig slop and the smell of the barbecue—both our need for grace and the forgiveness of God found in Jesus Christ. We must never get so far away from those smells that we forget how to extend forgiveness to others and be a part of fulfilling, biblical community. Although it does not negate our poor choice or save us from the ramifications, we must also recognize that we must forgive ourselves to be truly free.

This week we talked about how biblical community is made up of broken people, and even though we are made holy by the blood of Jesus, we all sometimes make "broken" choices—we speak unkindly, we act unfairly, we give grace unequally. Living in community with other believers can be challenging, no doubt, but biblical community is a gift. And it is worth the hard work of embracing forgiveness and extending it to others in order to keep the body of Christ healthy.

In our memory verse for this week, the apostle Paul, writing to the church at Colossae, says: "Bear with each other and forgive one another if any of you has a grievance against someone. Forgive as the Lord forgave you" (Colossians 3:13). The phrase "Forgive as the Lord forgave you" is key to helping us grasp what it means to forgive others. Before we even knew we needed forgiveness, Christ died to erase our sins. He models for us a lavish forgiveness, and when we can extend that kind of forgiveness to others (though it will surely never be perfect!), we can thrive in harmony with one another. Lavish forgiveness does not, however, excuse or overlook wrong, nor does it eliminate consequences.

Harmony is necessary in the body of Christ because we are a choir of sorts. We all have different parts to sing, we have a Conductor, and we are called to work together in the best interests of the choir. And when there are choir members who are not stars, who can barely hold their notes, we are called to associate with them and help them—and that means we also allow people to help us when we are the ones struggling. Harmony in the church is never perfect, but it is beautiful.

Though living in harmony with one another does not mean we have to agree on everything, as believers in Christ, we are united on the idea that Jesus is the Son of God, that He died on the cross and rose on the third day, that He lived a sinless life and conquered sin and death. Even when our opinions differ (and, oh, they will), we must continually come back to the common ground of Jesus; He is enough to unite us.

Lastly, in order to fully embrace our roles in biblical community, we must be willing and open to share ourselves—our gifts, strengths, stories, and wounds. But in order to do that, we must not only be kind and compassionate to one another; we need to be kind and compassionate to ourselves, willing to allow God to use our mistakes and shortcomings to point others to the One who is able to make all things new. Because Jesus is in the business of taking what we have to offer and making something beautiful and harmonious out of our mess.

Forgive One Another

Forgiveness Through the Lens of Biblical Community

> We can thrive in biblical community when we pursue peace, forgiveness, and restoration with God and others.

Welcome/Prayer/Icebreaker (5–10 minutes)

Welcome to Session 3 of *The Belonging Project: Finding Your Tribe and Learning to Thrive*. This week we've considered how biblical community is made up of broken people, and even though we are made holy by the blood of Jesus, we all sometimes make "broken" choices. Living in community with other believers can be challenging, but biblical community is a gift, and it is worth the hard work of embracing forgiveness and extending it to others in order to keep the body of Christ healthy. Today we'll explore what it looks like to pursue forgiveness in biblical community.

Take a moment to open with prayer, and then go around the circle and have each person complete this statement: Forgiveness is _____.

Video (about 20 minutes)

Play the video segment for Week 3, filling in the blanks as you watch and making notes about anything that resonates with you or that you want to be sure to remember.

—Video Notes—

Scripture Focus: Joshua 1:9; 2 Corinthians 13:11-12

A_____ for restoration.

A_____ with one another.

"_____" snare

"It's not _____" snare

"Is God even _____?" snare

A_____ to peace.

A_____ and give grace.

"Greet one another with a holy kiss." (2 Corinthians 13:12)

Other Insights:

Group Discussion (20–25 minutes for a 60-minute session; 30–35 minutes for a 90-minute session)

Video Discussion

- When you are struggling, which "snare" (see video notes above) tends to trip you up?
- Which of the four A's (see video notes above) resonates most with you right now?
- Good community does not mean we do not disagree; it means we cling to the things about which we *do* agree. As believers in Christ, what are some things we all can we agree on?

Workbook Discussion

- Read Romans 5:8 aloud. How did God demonstrate His love for us? (page 86) What does this tell us about how we are called to forgive others?
- In what areas of your life have you seen God redeem a hurt or an injustice? (page 84)
- Can you recall a time when you wanted to spoon out mercy rather than give it in shovelfuls? How did your refusal of grace affect the other party? How did it affect you? (page 90)
- Read James 5:16 aloud. According to this verse, what happens when we confess our sins and pray for one another? (page 92)
- What does Jesus say in Matthew 9:10-17 about how to treat others who might be considered "of low position"? What about this verse resonates with you the most? (page 98)
- Romans 3:23-24 tells us why harmony among believers will never be perfect. What are the challenges for biblical community, and what is our hope? (page 99)
- What role should forgiveness play in our unity with other believers? How important do you think it is? (page 103)
- Look up John 17:20-23. What is Jesus's prayer for those who believe in Him? Why do you think it so important for the body of Christ to be united? (page 104)

- Do you have a hard time forgiving yourself? What does Lamentations 3:22-23 say to you about how the Lord sees our mistakes? (page 108)

Connection Point (10–15 minutes—90 minute session only)

Divide into groups of two to three and discuss the following:

- Where is God leading you to extend forgiveness to another? What next steps do you need to take? (page 87)
- How is God prompting you to think or live differently as a result of what you've heard or learned this week?

Closing Prayer (5 minutes)

Close the session by sharing personal prayer requests and praying together. If you like, invite the women to surround those who have shared requests and pray for them aloud. In addition to praying aloud for one another, close by asking God to help you live out your desire to pursue forgiveness and peace, and for restoration among your community of believers.

Week 4

Fortify One Another

Exhortation Through the Lens of Biblical Community

Memory Verse

Let the message of Christ dwell among you richly as you teach and admonish one another with all wisdom through psalms, hymns, and songs from the Spirit, singing to God with gratitude in your hearts.

(Colossians 3:16)

Day 1: Directionally Challenged

Scripture
Focus

John 15:5-8

Today's "One Another"

Let the message of Christ dwell among you richly as you teach and admonish one another with all wisdom through psalms, hymns, and songs from the Spirit, singing to God with gratitude in your hearts."

(Colossians 3:16)

Years ago, I drove to visit my mom while she was nearby on a business trip. She lived about three hundred miles away, so I was excited when she called to say she'd be staying in a town only forty miles from my home. I drove over to visit her that Saturday morning, and planned to leave early the next morning to head back to our home church. My husband and I had been asked to sing in Sunday's church services, so I knew I needed to get there early.

Now this was back in the days when cell phones were the size of forearms and way too expensive for a newlywed couple in ministry. So, no cute little smart phone or GPS for me. I was unfamiliar with the area, so my mom suggested I speak with the concierge to get directions home before I left. The concierge had the most beautiful accent. It almost sounded as though he was singing as he gave a series of instructions, each followed by, "You cannot miss it." With each direction, "You cannot miss it." Each freeway exit, "You cannot miss it." Each landmark, "You cannot miss it."

Well, as you might have guessed, I missed it all right.

When I realized I was lost, the first place I pulled over was at a truck stop. When I approached two men to ask for directions, one of them looked me over like he was a kid in a candy shop and offered to drive me there himself. I freaked out. I panicked. I got back in the car and I drove even farther in the wrong direction.

When my heart rate finally returned to a normal pace, I ventured to ask for help again. This time, I stopped at a convenience store. The polite clerk gave me directions. Fortunately, she never said, "You cannot miss it." I got back on the freeway. I knew I was going to be late for church but there was no way to contact my husband (no cell phones, remember?). I pressed the gas pedal harder.

I kept waiting to see the signs the clerk had told me about, but they never came. Instead, there were signs for other cities I was not interested in. When I finally saw the name of a town I recognized, I realized I had gone about one hundred miles out of my way.

I pulled over at a rest stop and began to cry. I'm confident that others at the rest stop heard my wailing, and one sweet man took pity on me. When he knocked on the window, I was surprised by the sound and may have indeed lost bladder control. But he had kind eyes. "Are you OK, miss?" he asked.

"I'm lost," I blubbered.

"Where are you going?"

"To church," I responded, and then I gave the name of the town. His eyes widened.

"Oh, sweetheart, you are lost."

Duh, I thought to myself as I blew my nose.

But what he did next was life giving for me. He took a highlighter and a paper map (yes, I am old) and highlighted the directions for me. And then he got into his car and asked me to follow him. He said he would drive me all the way to the freeway to get me going in the right direction.

My sobbing subsided, I wiped off as much mascara as possible from underneath my eyes, took a deep breath, and followed him. He gave three quick honks when I was headed in the right direction and then waved wildly. I waved back. I was so thankful.

When I finally arrived at the church, they were halfway through the second service. I missed singing in church that day, but I did not miss the lesson taught to me by a stranger at a rest stop. That sweet man taught me a lot about going out of one's way to care for others, and maybe even about helping others find their way when they are lost.

**In what ways are you gifted in encouraging others?
What is your go-to move when you see someone who
might need a pick-me-up?**

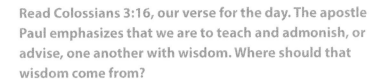

Read Colossians 3:16, our verse for the day. The apostle Paul emphasizes that we are to teach and admonish, or advise, one another with wisdom. Where should that wisdom come from?

Do you consider yourself to have the gift of teaching? If so, how can you embrace Paul's words? If not, what encouragement can you take from his words?

Today's "One Another" promotes teaching and admonishing one another as a natural progression. First, allow the Word of God to fill you so that you may, in turn, instruct and be instructed, encourage and be encouraged. Then give thanks to God for the process.

In order for us to embrace this teaching, we must spend time in God's Word and allow it to permeate who we are, how we think, and how we treat others. Then, in order to thrive in biblical community, we must be both teachable and willing to teach; grateful, and willing to give God the praise He deserves.

Read Jesus's words to us in John 15:5-8. What do we need to do in order to grow and be healthy?

What are some ways we can "remain" in Christ?

Has there been a season in your life where you were surviving on your own and disconnected from Jesus? What did life look like for you then?

Jesus says, "Apart from me you can do nothing" (v. 5). What is your reaction to that statement?

My husband and I were married almost nine years before we had our first child. We spent many years praying and hoping we would get pregnant, but it proved much more difficult than we had envisioned. When many, many months of "trying" passed and, despite the intercession of God's people, various ovulation tests, and a plethora of charts, it still wasn't happening, the little old ladies in our church started asking embarrassing questions like, "Is your husband a boxer or briefs guy?" or "Have you guys tried . . . ?"

When we finally got pregnant and I stayed that way through the first trimester, I did not think my heart could be any more full of joy. I had experienced a few miscarriages before, but when we got the thumbs-up from our doctor, we thought we were in the clear. We traveled home to tell our parents and celebrated together. After all those years, we were going to have a baby.

But the next day our hopes were dashed. We were visiting good friends at their church and I went into the restroom. I can only describe the next minutes by saying that there was pain, loss, and devastation all

at once. I screamed and cried from the restroom for a while, but no one heard me. I was in the middle of the house of God, yet I felt alone.

That event became the single greatest lesson in our lives as people in full-time ministry. My husband is the son of a pastor and a marriage and family counselor. He watched his parents pour into hundreds of people in crisis. He was very trained in how to minister to people. But nothing prepared him for this loss. Back at Bible college, we had been encouraged to memorize a plethora of Scriptures to fit different situations of ministry, but in that season, I found that what I needed to hear was not "In all things God works for the good of those who love him, who have been called according to his purpose" (Romans 8:28). In fact, to be honest, sometimes the Sword of Truth (God's Word) felt like a dagger in my heart when people flung it at me in an attempt to encourage us. What I needed was a hug. Someone to just sit with me in my sadness.

> **When you see someone in pain or in a difficult situation, how do you tend to respond? What actions do you tend to take?**

> **How can the time we spend "remaining" in Christ help us to best respond to and encourage people who are hurting?**

If we are to "let the message of Christ dwell among [us] richly" and encourage others, a couple of things need to happen. The first thing is we need to know the message of Christ. We need to become accustomed to spending time with Him and memorizing His Word. We need to celebrate the hope found in Scripture on a regular basis.

The second thing is we need to learn to "let," to let go and let God, as the saying goes. Often it takes a really difficult, trying season to open our eyes and let God move and let Him have our hearts and our lives. To let Him take control and teach others through us.

What disciplines do you practice to stay connected to God's Word?

The scale is often an indicator of how well I "live" healthy eating. The gas light is often an indicator of how well I pay attention to the gas level in my vehicle. Likewise, my ability to encourage others wholeheartedly, from a healthy place, is often an indicator of how much time I am spending in God's Word. My guess is that's true for you, too. When we let God's message "dwell" in our calendars, our priorities, and our focus, His love dwells also in the way that we care for others.

Call to Action

- Take a day, or a few hours, and unplug from your world as much as possible, allowing for some "remain" and "let" time.
- Spend time reading God's Word and listening to God. Find a quiet place, go for a walk, or listen to some praise music. However you choose to do it, make intentional space for talking with God.
- As you spend time with the Lord, ask if there is anyone who needs you to show up and just "let" them be where they are in their circumstance. Purposefully put aside your own agenda and what you think he or she may need, and instead pray for guidance about how best to love and support that person.
- Tell your pastor, clergy, or mentors how much you appreciate them serving your community and acknowledge that they have a tough job to do. Pray for them as they navigate the ups and downs of their own lives.

Day 2: Daily Encouragement

Today's "One Another"

But encourage one another daily, as long as it is called "Today," so that none of you may be hardened by sin's deceitfulness.

(Hebrews 3:13)

Scripture Focus

Genesis 3:1-7

Just so you know, I am a terrible artist. Like, the worst. I cannot even draw stick figures; my stick figures often have additional lines. I mean, if dancing to eighties music or embarrassing one's kids was an art, I would be a master, but I don't think those things count. I tried sculpture in school. What started off as a vase ended up being the world's most hideous glasses holder. It was an epic fail. My mom still has it somewhere in her home, but I have asked her to put it away to avoid scaring small children and the elderly.

That being said, I really admire true artists. Painters, sculptors, photographers, architects, as well as other artists of other forms amaze and inspire me. Dale Chihuly is one of my favorites. His sculptures are in glass—not like those small glassblower figurine shops that one often finds in tourist towns. They are complex and narrative in nature.

Chihuly has had a long, illustrious career, an extensive education, and his works span the globe in museums, botanical gardens, aquariums, and in the lobby of the Bellagio Hotel in Las Vegas. But something happened in 1976 that changed his life forever. He was involved in a head-on collision, propelled through the front windshield, and severely cut by the glass. Due to the accident, Chihuly was blinded in his left eye permanently.

The very thing that is the medium for his work, glass, was the very thing that diminished his sight. If it were me, I would search for the most fashionable pirate-eye patch in history and find another hobby, but not Chihuly. He continued in his passion; but from that point forward, the artist had to rely heavily on assistant glassblowers, called gaffers, to help him create his masterpieces. Then, three years after the accident, Chihuly dislocated his right shoulder bodysurfing, which prevented him from properly holding the tools necessary for creating his distinct pieces. He had to lean even more heavily into the gaffers to keep up with the growing demand.

When interviewed, Chihuly admitted that these injuries actually proved advantageous. As he supervised and directed the gaffers, he was able to view the burgeoning pieces from more angles and anticipate problematic issues earlier in the process. He described his new role this way: "I am more choreographer than dancer, more supervisor than participant, more director than actor." Chihuly is a very wealthy and successful man, but his gaffers have proved themselves invaluable. They have enabled his business, his art, his reach, and his impact on the world to continue.[1]

I want to be a gaffer when I grow up—not for Dale Chihuly, but for those God has placed in my path. I want to be a person who comes alongside and helps someone see things from a different perspective, who makes others more effective, helps them see issues that might arise, and practically maneuvers through those issues in a beautiful and meaningful way.

> **Do you have a gaffer—a person who encourages you and helps you make things happen? If so, what has he or she done for you?**

> **In what ways have you done the same for someone else? What did you learn from your experience in supporting another person's efforts or dreams?**

I consider myself a gaffer of sorts when it comes to clothes shopping and looking out for other women, because I hate it when I am out shopping, spot something adorable, and then realize that someone has placed an item *in the wrong size section*. Of course that shirt is adorable. It is a size 0! Everything is adorable in that size. My arm would look awesome in it! When this happens to me, I put the garment back in the right place so that the next woman shopping in the not-size-0 section will not be discouraged, as I was. (See? I am here to serve!)

Similarly, when we take the time and effort to encourage one another in Jesus, we are encouraged in our spiritual walk too.

Today's "One Another," Hebrews 3:13, tells us to "encourage one another daily." I don't know about you, but I am pretty good at executing my weekly responsibilities. And I am quite fantastic with monthly obligations. But daily? I even can't remember what I had for lunch today. (Oh wait, yes I do. It was delicious.) Practicing something daily takes some time to develop into a habit, but when one puts in the time, the payoff can be big.

> **What are some ways you can commit to daily encouragement of others (such as your family or your coworkers)?**

> **What are some ways you might encourage yourself each day, remembering God's love for and faithfulness to you?**

Hebrews 3:13 continues, saying that we should "encourage one another daily...so that none of you may be hardened by sin's deceitfulness." Sin, which can so easily creep into our hearts, can really do a number on us. We don't have to look very far into the Bible to see what it looks like to be deceived by sin and then hardened by its consequences.

> **Read Genesis 3:1-7. How did Satan (disguised as a serpent) deceive Eve, and then Adam? What lie did he plant in their hearts?**

How did Adam and Eve act toward the Lord as a result of their sin?

When have you been deceived by sin? What effect did it have on your relationship with God? with others?

The bad news is that Satan lives for trying to deceive us and separate us from God. And he is pretty relentless about it too. But the good news—the amazing, fantastic, life-changing news—is that because of Jesus's death on the cross, Satan can never separate us from God's love. He may tempt us and mess with us, and sometimes we'll fall for it; but that doesn't change the fact that we are God's children and that His love for us is secure and never-ending.

These are the words we need to hear *daily*—and that we need to proclaim over one another on a regular basis. We desperately need these reminders so that we don't get caught up in our discouragement or caught up in sin that can so easily harden our hearts. We need to know that Jesus is there for us and is the only one who can truly relieve the burden of sin.

Look up the following verses, and write down a phrase from each one that resonates with you, something you can use as a daily reminder of what Jesus has done for you.

Romans 8:28

Romans 8:1-2

John 3:16-17

Call to Action

- Pray that God would fill your days with opportunities to encourage others and to be a "gaffer" for them.
- If we are going to find our tribe and learn to thrive, we need to be committed to encourage others. Not the "Oh my, what a cute dress!" encouragement (although that is always fun—not the wearing a dress part, but the compliment part), but the encouragement of others in their walk with Jesus. How can you encourage someone in his or her spiritual walk today?
- We live in a discouraging world. The political climate, the tragedies all over the nation, the starvation of children all over the world, the disregard of the value of human life, the threat of war, the rise in stress and anxiety—it is overwhelming. How do we keep our perspective? By focusing on Jesus and encouraging one another daily. Do one small thing today to encourage another believer.
- Are you discouraged today, or feeling the weight of sin? If you have someone with whom you can share your burdens, someone you can not only encourage but also receive encouragement from, reach out to that person today and let them know how you're feeling.

Day 3: Rooted and Established in Community

Today's "One Another"

²⁴*And let us consider how we may spur one another on toward love and good deeds,* ²⁵*not giving up meeting together, as some are in the habit of doing, but encouraging one another—and all the more as you see the Day approaching.*

(Hebrews 10:24-25)

Today I ate my first tomato of the season. You see, this was a big deal because, of all the gifts that God gave me, the ability to care for and keep plants alive is not on the list. Every season I cash in on that guarantee that hardware stores offer for plants purchased at their stores—if the plants die, the stores will replace them. I always keep my receipt because I know I will need it before the season ends. I am confident that plants hear Darth Vader's "Imperial Death March" when I enter the store. I'll bet if they could run and hide, they would. But earlier this year I committed myself to doing the very best I could to have successful tomato plants. I watered, battled aphids, nurtured, added nutrients, sang over them, and today I got to enjoy the fruits of my labor. And it was glorious.

My mother is a master with all things green, but my husband's grandmother was probably the most proficient gardener I have ever met. Grandma DeFriend was a force to be reckoned with. She was a kind, loving, jovial woman who loved her family, pinochle, and spending time in the garden. She told the story about how, when they moved into their house outside of San Diego, there was a beautiful garden out back with a gorgeous tree in the very middle. The leaves looked like those of a citrus tree, although there was no fruit on it, so she wasn't sure what kind it was.

Grandma was determined for that tree to bear fruit, though, so she read everything she could about how to encourage fruit-bearing trees. She tried every method in the book, to no avail. So, naturally, she contacted the Department of Agriculture in California. I did not know that the Department of Agriculture took phone calls, but knowing Grandma, even if they didn't, they would have made an exception for her. She spoke to a

woman who gave her suggestions on what to try next, but Grandma had already tried them all. So she asked to speak to the woman's manager. (First of all, I would *never* think to call the Department of Agriculture, and I certainly would never think to ask if the person with whom I was speaking had a manager I could talk to! I told you she was exceptional.) The manager reluctantly told her there was only one other idea he had; he told her to take a broom and to hit the bottom of that tree as hard as she could, as close to the ground as possible. He gave her permission to take out all of her frustrations on that tree, giving it all she had.

So she did. She let that tree have it! And wouldn't you know, the next season that tree produced more oranges than they could consume! It seems it was a perfectly healthy tree, but the roots needed to be stimulated so the tree could produce fruit.

I think the same thing sometimes happens with us. We can look healthy on the outside, but sometimes it takes a few hard hits to shake us out of our comfort zone and get us going again. In fact, I've found that it is often those seasons of tumult that produce the most amazing "fruit" in our lives.

Has there been a time in your life when your roots were beaten, so to speak? How did that season change you or challenge you?

How was your faith changed or challenged? What do you think God taught you during that time?

Though hard times can produce good fruit, we can be grateful we don't always have to be in a really hard season in order to grow and flourish. Our "roots" can be awakened and stimulated by others around us who encourage us to grow in ways that are beneficial and fruitful—and, dare I say, even fun?

For example, I actually love going to the gym. I don't enjoy the tight clothes (Lord, have mercy) or the getting up early part (*blech*), but I love the feeling of accomplishment I have when I am done with a workout. Also, at my gym I am like Norm from *Cheers*. Everyone knows my name. I give high fives and do my best to speak to as many people as I can. I might be thinner if I exercised the muscles in my legs as much as I do those of my mouth, but that is not the point.

I am most faithful at the gym when I have a half-marathon, triathlon, or major running event coming up. I will let others at the gym know the reason for my extra training, and they often use that to encourage me to train better so I am ready for the big race day. As the day of the race gets closer, my need for encouragement increases.

When I don't show up, people notice. Sometimes I get texts saying, "We missed you today" or "Are you OK?" I also text others when I do not see them, not to make them feel bad for skipping the gym, but because I care about those folks. They see me without makeup, sweaty, and in eighties headbands, but they still like me! Crazy!

It costs me to be a member of the gym, but the value outweighs the cost. It reminds me of the church. And as members of the church, it is not healthy for believers to give up the strengthening we receive from meeting together, giving one another high fives (OK, just metaphorically at my church), holding one another accountable, and reminding the members how valuable they are.

It costs to be a part of such a group. It costs our time, our vulnerability, our dedication, our prayers, and our pride. But we are important to one another. We are called to serve, give, love, and to remind one another of the Big Event coming up—the approaching day when Jesus returns. With that in mind, we are well served to encourage other believers to be prepared, serve harder, and love more deeply.

Sometimes, just like going to the gym, we get out of the habit of meeting together. And when a brother or sister in Christ gives up meeting with others, it costs us kindness, concern, and love to remind that person

just how important he or she is to the group—not out of judgment, but out of a genuine concern for that person. For us to be brought into the family of God and have fellowship with one another cost Jesus His life. Let's count that cost and choose to encourage one another to keep our focus on Jesus. In doing so, we will also be strengthened and encouraged.

What does Hebrews 10:24-25 say meeting together does for us as believers? Why should we even go to church?

Are you in a habit of being part of a body of believers? What are the costs? What are the benefits?

What are the obstacles of "meeting regularly"? Why is consistency in this important?

Have you ever been tempted to give up biblical community? If so, what happened, and what did God teach you during that time?

Living in regular biblical community helps us grow, but that growth can be painful. Sometimes growing in maturity and wisdom can feel as though Grandma is beating our roots, so to speak. But when we do face difficult times, we can know that God has all power and ability to bring about amazing "fruit" and growth, even in our discomfort.

Read 2 Corinthians 4:16-18 in the margin. How does this verse encourage or challenge you to think about difficult times in life?

Just as suffering through hard seasons can produce good fruit in our lives, so does the practice of thankfulness. I'm so thankful for the people in my life who have challenged me to take time to give God thanks for what He's given me. As I began focusing my awareness on the things that God has done for me, I saw how that gratefulness began to bear fruit in my life. I find myself more content with the things I have and less focused on the things I don't. I'm recognizing that I'm spending less time comparing myself to others. And I feel more joyful, even when circumstances don't change.

One way we can encourage one another in our walk with Christ is to learn to live in gratitude for what he has done for us—and for what He has given us in one another.

Read the apostle Paul's words to the church at Corinth in 1 Corinthians 1:4. What was Paul grateful for, and what effect do you think his words had on the Corinthian believers?

Name one person in your life whom you are grateful for. What has this person added to your life? What has he or she taught you about God?

Read Psalm 106:1. This is a simple verse with great meaning. Below write a prayer of thanksgiving to God for who He is and what He has done for you.

Thankfulness is easy to see the benefits of—and hard to practice. Opening one's eyes to the beauty and awesomeness of the things around us takes intention, but the fruits are contentment, deep-abiding joy, and encouragement to those around you. Gratitude fosters community and inspires your tribe to do likewise.

Call to Action

- If you are not part of a church, commit to spending time to find a body in which you can grow in your knowledge of God's Word, stretch your faith muscles, and be built up by other believers.
- If God leads you to do so, consider encouraging with a text, call, email, or letter someone you know who has left the church.
- Develop a habit of gratitude through daily practice—perhaps by writing down all the things you are thankful for each day, speaking them aloud in prayer, or finding another way to express your thanks to God.
- Thank the people in your life who spur you on and encourage you to grow. Let them know how God has blessed you because of them.

Day 4: Being Shell-fish

Scripture Focus

Ruth 1-3

Today's "One Another"

You, my brothers and sisters, were called to be free. But do not use your freedom to indulge the flesh; rather, serve one another humbly in love.

(Galatians 5:13)

If I could eat only one food for a year, it would be Dungeness crab. (Yes, every story I tell goes back to food. Don't judge.) Give me a little bit of sauce, a couple of tools, a ton of napkins, and back away slowly.

Dungeness crabs are a big deal in Northern California, where I grew up. This type of crab looks more like a muscular wrestler than a tall basketball player and the meat is sweet and delightful.

I love to eat them, but I do not want to hang out with them.

I read recently that crabs have an interesting way of operating when it comes to their friends. The reputation for their behavior is so bad, there is actually a phrase to describe their behavior: "crab mentality" or "crabs in a bucket mentality."[2] When crabs are trapped in a bucket, if one tries to climb out, the other crabs will pull it back down. The ironic part of this is that because of this mentality, no crab escapes; they all meet their doom, especially in my kitchen. Simply put, crab mentality is one or more crab wanting to keep one's peers down in order for that crab to succeed itself (or at least not to fail). And if they cannot succeed, they feel no remorse in making sure no other crab does either.

Some humans suffer from this mentality too. Although they may not physically pull a person down for attempting to "rise above," some people try to erode another person's self-assuredness or undermine their success in order to keep them down. Sadly, whether they know it or not, it drags them down as well. This happens in schools too. According to a study in New Zealand in 2015, there is a marked difference (up to an 18 percent average increase) in exam scores when other students in the class were kept from knowing each individual's ranking in the class.[3] When each person no longer feared what others might say about the test scores because the results were presented anonymously, the scores increased.

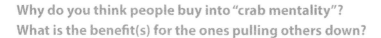

Why do you think people buy into "crab mentality"?
What is the benefit(s) for the ones pulling others down?

Have you ever felt that someone was purposefully
trying to hold you back or pull you down? What
happened and what effect did it have on you?

One of the most inspiring stories in the Bible is the story of Ruth. No one is farther from "crab mentality" than our good friend Ruth.

The Book of Ruth opens with the story of Naomi, an Israelite woman who moved to Moab with her husband and two sons in order to escape famine. After moving there, Naomi's husband died. Her two sons married Moabite women—Ruth and Orpah—but then both sons died, leaving their mother and their widows to figure out what to do next.

Naomi wanted to return to her homeland (Bethlehem), and so she encouraged her daughters-in-law to leave her and return to their families and to find new husbands. Orpah went home, but Ruth choose to go with Naomi back to Bethlehem. This was a big deal. Ruth chose to go to a foreign land with her mother-in-law, turning away from all she had known to follow the God of her husband.

Let me pause a moment and say that although my mother-in-law was a wonderful woman, I am not sure I would have been able to make that choice. And I am confident that she would have done more than insist that I go home and return to my people had we faced that situation!

(Just in case, I am praying for my kids' future spouses—that they would not want to sell me on Ebay one day when they are stuck with me!)

Read Ruth 1:15-18. What strikes you most about this story?

Imagine you were in Ruth's shoes. Why do you think Ruth chooses to stay with Naomi? (No wrong answers here! We don't have much information about their relationship to go on.)

Read a little further in Ruth 1, verses 20-21. What state was Naomi in at this point in her life? How do you imagine Ruth's choice affected her?

We don't really know why Ruth made the choice she made, but we do know that God blessed her faithfulness and had a wonderful plan for her life. She married one of Naomi's relatives, Boaz, which guaranteed that she and Naomi would be well taken care of. She became a mother and an ancestor of our Lord Jesus—in fact, she is one of only five women mentioned in His ancestry (see Matthew 1). In addition, hers is one of only two books of the Bible named after a woman (the other one is Esther). Through her humility and lack of "crab mentality," God honored Ruth and placed her in a position of honor.

What encouragement do you draw from Ruth's story?

Ruth certainly set an example for us that beautifully illustrates the truths in Galatians 5:13, our verse for today, despite the fact that the Book of Galatians was written thousands of years after Ruth lived on earth.

Galatians 5:13 begins, "You, my brothers and sisters, were called to be free." Although she had all rights and privileges to go back home, Ruth showed faith by following Naomi to a new land. She found "freedom" in community and a new life in Bethlehem.

The verse continues, "but do not use your freedom to indulge the flesh; rather, serve one another humbly in love." Left to our own devices, we are a selfish people. Without Jesus, we would certainly be tempted to "indulge the flesh" and practice crab mentality. But Christ followers are "called to be free," and because of that freedom we are to serve one another with humility and love. And there is nothing closer to the heart of Jesus than our service to others. It shows the world that we live not to pull others down but to lift up the name of Jesus.

Ruth's goal was to honor her late husband and her new God by humbly serving Naomi. Serving humbly means to serve without expecting anything in return. It means showing love by neither demanding or impatiently waiting for gratitude. Because of her humility and love, Ruth was blessed with a new community and a rediscovered hope.

Has there been a time in your life when your willingness to serve another gave you fresh community and renewed hope? If so, what were the circumstances of that experience?

Ruth stepped out of her comfort zone into an unfamiliar culture. Where might God be calling you out of your comfort in order to serve another?

Ruth served Naomi during a really difficult time in both their lives. Who might God be calling you to walk alongside and serve during a difficult time in their lives?

Leaving the comfort of our busy schedules and regular patterns can be downright daunting, but just like Ruth, we may be blessed for our willingness to follow God into new territories. If we are to make new connections and make a difference in the lives of others, we need to be willing to step out in faith and follow God, serve others, and live in the biblical community to which He has called us.

Call to Action

- Make a list of small, practical ways you could serve others. Consider the things you do well, your gifts, and your resource of time; it is much easier to serve others out of the gifts God has given us.
- Pray about where God is calling you to serve others, and when He answers you, move forward with that call, even if you only take a small step. You might even want to tell a trusted friend about where you feel led in order to have some encouragement and accountability.

Scripture Focus

Hebrews 12:1;
Romans 12:6-10;
Hebrews 12:1

Day 5: Encouragement on Wheels

Today's "One Another"

[14]For we believe that Jesus died and rose again, and so we believe that God will bring with Jesus those who have fallen asleep in him. . . . [18]Therefore encourage one another with these words.

(1 Thessalonians 4:14, 18)

My sister, Allyson, is my person. What I mean by that is that she knows more about me than any other human on the planet and she chooses to like me anyway. She is wickedly smart, funny, beautiful, and thinner than I am. If I did not really love her, I would hate her.

For many years, my sister participated in the MS 150, a fundraiser for multiple sclerosis that included a 150-mile bike ride. She's always been athletic, and I marveled at her ability to complete these bike races. Just getting those tight, padded, biking shorts over my hindquarters is enough to discourage me from such a task. But I digress.

When I asked her what moved her to participate in such a thing (as far as I knew, she didn't know anybody who has had MS), she said a friend convinced her to do it once; and after the first experience, she didn't want to miss it. You see, for the last ten miles of the race, friends and family of people with MS and those afflicted with the crippling disease line the streets. And for each of those miles, they cheer, clap, and, sometimes scream in gratitude toward the people participating in the fundraiser. They're so thankful for these individuals willing to raise large amounts of money for MS, and they eagerly anticipate the opportunity to thank the cyclists and philanthropists. My sister said that it was so moving the first year, she cried so hard she thought she was going to run somebody over with her bike. It was a life-changing experience for her.

A few years later I talked her into doing a three-day walk for breast cancer. I had known plenty of people with breast cancer and had a friend who had recently gone through it, so I talked my sister into walking with me. I was in no shape to walk sixty miles; I was in no shape to walk six miles, but I trained. I prepared. However, in no way can going to the gym a couple of days a week prepare one's feet for walking sixty miles in three days.

The other walkers were so encouraging. Many participants donned shirts in memory of the person for whom they were walking. Some families would walk for a family member, and their T-shirts and banners reflected accordingly. The restaurants in the area would celebrate those who were walking and would sometimes even cheer as we walked by. I nearly lost bladder control a couple of times when, unexpectedly, a car would honk in encouragement. The local community was wonderful, and it was as meaningful to me as anything I've ever done. I felt I was an integral part of the community while surrounded by thousands of complete strangers. But we had a goal in mind. We had a purpose. And we felt strongly that it was our job to encourage one another. Even if my feet wanted to file for divorce after the sixty miles, my heart felt so full.

How would our towns, our country, and our world be different if the church was known for its encouragement to others? Instead of being known for the issues we stand for on Facebook, what if we were known for truly encouraging other people?

The word *encourage* comes from an Old French word meaning "make strong, hearten."[4] I cannot imagine the impact on the world if you and I consistently "heartened" the people in our community who need it the most. What would happen if we spoke less and loved more?

Have you ever accomplished a goal you did not know was possible? Who encouraged you in that goal?

When have you witnessed a church body or group of believers showing up big to celebrate or encourage others in some way? What impact did it have on your community?

In grade school, I was often the largest and tallest girl in my class, sometimes by a full foot. When teams were chosen in PE class, if the game we were playing called for sheer mass, I was often the first picked. However, if the game needed speed, I was often one of the last to be chosen. I remember the painful feelings when the team captain's eyes would pass over me and find the better choice in another. It hurt not to be chosen.

In order to work on my skills in each of the sports, I would often stay after school for a few minutes and practice. I did not think anyone noticed, but during a particularly painful team choosing, my PE teacher

leaned over and said, "Be patient. In a few years, with all the practice you are putting in, your skills will catch up with your height and you will be unstoppable."

It was just the encouragement I needed. I stayed after school almost every day that year and practiced. I started being picked earlier in the rounds, and other students began to recognize the fruits of my effort.

Can you recall a time when you were struggling and God sent someone to encourage you to press on?

Read Hebrews 12:1 in the margin. How does this Scripture encourage you in your walk with Christ?

Therefore, since we are surrounded by such a huge crowd of witnesses to the life of faith, let us strip off every weight that slows us down, especially the sin that so easily trips us up. And let us run with endurance the race God has set before us.
(Hebrews 12:1 NLT)

Just like my PE teacher did, we can come alongside one another and whisper encouragement about the good news of Jesus. (Shouting is also perfectly acceptable; I am a loud person by nature and I do not whisper well. Even my whispers are obnoxious.) We can remind one another that we serve a risen Savior, and that news alone should give us hope for the present and the future. We also can encourage one another with the promise of heaven and the perspective it provides.

Read Today's "One Another," 1 Thessalonians 4:14-18. As believers, what is our hope based on?

How does the promise of heaven, or eternal life, encourage you in your daily life?

Something in us desires to be part of something greater, and I truly believe that desire is a gift from God. This includes the gift of desire to be in community with other believers. We were designed for that kind of community, but it takes lots of work, patience, and encouragement to find it and to maintain it.

I don't think I've ever met someone who doesn't love to be encouraged, and I am confident that encouraging others has a high ROI (return on investment). It costs little to nothing to give, and it reaps huge rewards when done consistently and sincerely. In order to truly thrive in our tribe, we must figure out how to encourage others using that which God has given us. For some, verbal affirmation is easy to give. For others, it is easy for them to make little gifts to give as encouragement. For some, giving others the gift of time and presence is their strength.

Read Romans 12:6-8. The apostle Paul points out that we are each uniquely gifted in different ways to serve the body of Christ. What do you think is a God-given strength of yours? (Hint: It doesn't have to be one of the ones listed in this verse. And if you have trouble identifying one, just ask a friend. He or she will be able to help!)

⁹Don't just pretend to love others. Really love them. Hate what is wrong. Hold tightly to what is good. ¹⁰Love each other with genuine affection, and take delight in honoring each other.
(Romans 12:9-10)
NLT

What encouragement do you draw from understanding that we all have different gifts and strengths and are equipped for different ways to serve?

Read Romans 12:9-10 in the margin. These verses basically encapsulate everything we have been

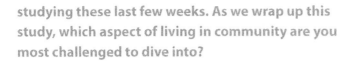

studying these last few weeks. As we wrap up this study, which aspect of living in community are you most challenged to dive into?

When I examine Romans 12:9-10, my eyes are immediately drawn to the verbs—"pretend to love," "love," "hate," "hold," "take delight," and "honor." It seems like so much work, and yet I feel like the words are instead instructing us to focus on the heart behind the verbs. We should not misuse or spend energy pretending. Instead, we should spend our time, strength, and lives loving genuinely. If we are going to find our tribe and learn to thrive, our love and actions need to be grounded in truth, not fiction.

Romans 12:9-10 begins with true love and includes a charge to be devoted to our biblical community with that love. When we live in biblical community, it takes a commitment to doing good, honoring others, and being humble—all keys to truly loving others, to learning to thrive.

Call to Action

- Make a list of people you know would benefit from some celebrations (couldn't we all?). Schedule some opportunities to celebrate the victories of others with a phone call, a high five, a meal, or a coffee and a donut (unless they are doing the Paleo diet, then get some of those Paleo ones, too).
- If you haven't already, identify your God-given strengths, and pray that God would reveal to you the best ways to celebrate those strengths and use them in service for others.

Weekly Wrap-up

Just like Chihuly needs his gaffers and I need my gym mates, we need others who come alongside us in our lives to encourage us, to remind us of why we're here, and to hold us up when we don't have the strength to go on.

Scripture has had so much to say to us this week about how to fortify and encourage one another. We've explored how we need the Word of God to fill us up so that we may in turn instruct and be instructed, encourage and be encouraged, and then give thanks to God for the process. We must spend time in God's Word and allow it to permeate who we are, how we think, and how we treat others. In order to thrive in biblical community, we must be both teachable and willing to teach, grateful and willing to give God the praise He deserves.

The burdens of life are real and heavy, and we need daily encouragement to hold strong and face our challenges. And when those challenges are daunting, we need others to come alongside us and remind us that sometimes the roots of our lives have to be "beaten" and our comfortable lives shaken so that the fruit can grow once again.

It costs to be a part of biblical community—it costs our time, our vulnerability, our dedication, our prayers, and our pride. But the cost is worth it. We are important to one another. We are called to serve, give, love, and remind one another of the Big Event coming up—the approaching day when Jesus returns. With that in mind, we are well served to encourage other believers to be prepared, serve harder, and love more deeply, to walk in the freedom of Christ's love for us, to live in the gifts He has so generously given us.

There is nothing closer to the heart of Jesus than our service to others. It shows the world that we live not to pull others down but to lift up the name of Jesus.

A Final Word

Recently, while on a zoo tour, I learned about wallowing. We were on a tour bus, passing the hippo exhibit, when the tour guide referred to the mud pit in which the hippo was laying in as a "wallow." I had never thought of *wallow* as a noun. I had always heard it as a verb. For example, "He was wallowing in self-pity." Or "She was wallowing in a hot fudge sundae after a long day."

So I asked the guide about the wallow. It seems that hippos, as well as some other animals, will submerge their bodies for a few reasons: to protect their skin from the sun, to keep themselves cool, and because

it is very comfortable for them. He went on to explain that a wallow is partially made of rainwater and dust, but for the most part, it consists of the waste from the animal. Ew. This makes me think of a marinade, the kind you use when you want to give your food more flavor. Marinating, however, is not about comfort. It is about permeating the submerged vegetable or meat and making it into something more delicious. It's about bringing out the flavor of the original food and elevating it into something extraordinary.

If we are to grow in biblical community, we must choose to marinate in God's Word because we're going to need what it has to give! Biblical community is not for the easily discouraged, but it is worth the work! In order to do it well, we need God's Word to dwell in us so that we can encourage one another, teach one another, praise God alongside one another, maintain unity, forgive others and ourselves, encourage one another, find our tribe, and learn to thrive.

We were made for community and connection. When we were created in the image of God, Who operates in community, we were made with a desire for healthy, loving community. And though we will certainly face challenges as we live with one another, God has given us the tools and encouragement we need to both survive and to thrive as members of the body of Christ. Community makes us stronger, strengthens our faith in Jesus, and makes us more like Him. God can use our desire to practice the "one anothers" to build community, make our lives in Him extraordinary, and encourage others as well. We honor Him and show the world just how awesome He is when we practice loving one another.

Fortify One Another
Exhortation Through the Lens of Biblical Community

> We can thrive in biblical community because God has given us the tools and encouragement we need.

Welcome/Prayer/Icebreaker (5–10 minutes)

Welcome to Session 4 of *The Belonging Project: Finding Your Tribe and Learning to Thrive*. This week we've explored how we need the Word of God to fill us up so that we may in turn instruct and be instructed, encourage, and be encouraged. In order to thrive in biblical community, we must be both teachable and willing to teach, grateful and willing to give God the praise He deserves. Today we'll explore what it looks like to support and encourage one another using the tools and the gifts God has already given us.

Take a moment to open with prayer, and then go around the circle and briefly identify a memorable time when someone gave you timely or effective words of encouragement or instruction.

Video (about 20 minutes)

Play the video segment for Week 4, filling in the blanks as you watch and making notes about anything that resonates with you or that you want to be sure to remember.

—Video Notes—

Scripture Focus: Romans 15:14

F_____

"You yourselves are full of _____."

F_____

"Filled with all _____."

F_____

"Able to _____ one another."

Other Insights:

Group Discussion (20–25 minutes for a 60-minute session; 30–35 minutes for a 90-minute session)

Video Discussion

- What is the difference between having knowledge about God and His Word and living that out? Why are both important?

- What does it mean to be a "sherpa" for others?
- When has someone been a safe place for you?

Workbook Discussion

- In what ways are you gifted in encouraging others? What is your go-to move when you see someone who might need a pick-me-up? (page 120)
- Read Jesus's words to us in John 15:5-8. What do we need to do in order to grow and be healthy? What are some ways we can "remain" in Christ? (pages 121-122)
- When have you been deceived by sin? What effect did it have on your relationship with God? With others? (page 128)
- What promise does God make to us in Romans 8:28? (see page 128)
- What does Hebrews 10:24-25 say meeting together does for us as believers? Why should we even go to church? (page 133)
- In what ways does biblical community encourage you?
- Has there been a time in your life when your willingness to serve another gave you fresh community and renewed hope? If so, what were the circumstances of that experience? (page 139)
- What encouragement do you draw from Ruth's story (with regards to living in community with other believers)? (page 138)
- How does Hebrews 12:1 encourage you in your walk with Christ? (page 143)
- Romans 12:9-10 basically encapsulates everything we have been studying these last few weeks. As we wrap up this study, which aspect of living in community are you most challenged to dive into? (pages 144-145)

Connection Point (10–15 minutes—90 minute session only)

Divide into groups of two to three and discuss the following:

- What strengths do you think God has given you? As you consider how God is calling you to dive more deeply into biblical community and your tribe, how might you use those strengths to love and serve others?

- How is God prompting you to think or live differently as a result of what you've heard or learned this week, or throughout this study?

Closing Prayer (5 minutes)

Close the session by thanking the group for journeying together in this study. Share personal prayer requests and pray together. If you like, invite the women to surround those who have shared requests and pray for them aloud. In addition to praying aloud for one another, close by thanking God for your time together and by praying God would guide us as we would continue to thrive in biblical community and be open to all that God is teaching us about loving and serving one another.

Leader Helps

Tips for Facilitating a Group

Important Information

Before the first session you will want to distribute copies of this study guide to the members of your group. Be sure to communicate that, if possible, they are to complete the first week in the study guide before your first group session. For each week there are personal lessons divided into five sections, or days, which participants may choose to complete each day or all at once depending on their schedules and preferences.

As you gather each week with the members of your group, you will have the opportunity to watch a video, discuss and respond to what you're learning, and pray together. You will need access to a television and DVD player with working remotes or a computer and monitor if you will be viewing streaming video files (available from Cokesbury.com and Amplifymedia.com). Use the Group Session Guide at the end of each week's lessons to facilitate the session (options are provided for both a 60-minute and 90-minute meeting time). In addition to these guides, the Group Session Guide Leader Notes (pages 155–158) provide additional helps including a main objective, key Scripture references, and overview for each session.

Creating a warm and inviting atmosphere will help to make the women feel welcome. Although optional, you might consider providing snacks for your first meeting and inviting group members to rotate in bringing refreshments each week.

As group leader, your role is to guide and encourage the women on the journey to finding and thriving in their tribe and living in true biblical community. Pray that God would pour out His Spirit on your time together, that the Spirit would speak into each woman's life and circumstances, and that your group would grow in community with one another.

Preparing for the Sessions

- Be sure to communicate dates and times to participants in advance.

- Make sure that group members have their workbooks at least one week before your first session and instruct them to complete the first week of personal lessons in the study guide. If you have the phone numbers or email addresses of your group members, send out a reminder and a welcome.
- Check out your meeting space before each group session. Make sure the room is ready. Do you have enough chairs? Do you have the equipment and supplies you need? (See the list of materials that follows.)
- Pray for your group and each group member by name. Ask God to work in the life of every woman in your group.
- Read and complete the week's readings in this study guide and review the group session guide. Select the discussion points and questions you want to make sure to cover during your time together, as there will be more information here than you will likely be able to cover in your session. You might want to make notes in the margins to share in your discussion time.

Leading the Sessions

- Personally welcome and greet each woman as she arrives. Take attendance if desired.
- In order to create a warm, welcoming environment as the women are gathering, consider either lighting one or more candles, providing coffee or other refreshments, or playing worship music, or all of these. (Bring an iPod, smartphone, or tablet and a portable speaker if desired.) Be sure to provide name tags if the women do not know one another or you have new participants in your group.
- Always start on time. Honor the time of those who are on time.
- At the start of each session, ask the women to turn off or silence their cell phones.
- Communicate the importance of completing the weekly lessons and participating in group discussion.
- Encourage everyone to participate fully, but don't put anyone on the spot. Invite the women to share as they are comfortable. Be prepared to offer a personal example or answer if no one else responds at first.
- Facilitate but don't dominate. Remember that if you talk most of the time, group members may tend to listen rather than to engage. Your task is to encourage conversation and keep the discussion moving.
- If someone monopolizes the conversation, kindly thank her for sharing and ask if anyone else has any insights.

- Try not to interrupt, judge, or minimize anyone's comments or input.
- Remember that you are not expected to be the expert or have all the answers. Acknowledge that all of you are on this journey together, with the Holy Spirit as your leader and guide. If issues or questions arise that you don't feel equipped to handle, talk with the pastor or a staff member at your church.
- Don't rush to fill the silence. If no one speaks right away, it's OK to wait for someone to answer. After a moment, ask, "Would anyone be willing to share?" If no one responds, try asking the question again a different way, or offer a brief response and ask if anyone has anything to add.
- Encourage good discussion, but don't be timid about calling time on a particular question and moving ahead. Part of your responsibility is to keep the group on track. If you decide to spend extra time on a given question or activity, consider skipping or spending less time on another question or activity in order to stay on schedule.
- Do your best to end on time. If you are running over, give members the opportunity to leave if they need to. Then wrap up as quickly as you can.
- Thank the women for coming and let them know you're looking forward to seeing them next time.
- Be prepared for some women to want to hang out and talk at the end. If you need everyone to leave by a certain time, communicate this at the beginning of the group session. If you are meeting in a church during regularly scheduled activities, be aware of nursery closing times.

Materials Needed

- *The Belonging Project* study guide with leader helps
- *The Belonging Project* DVD and a DVD player, or a computer and monitor
- Stick-on name tags and markers (optional)
- iPod, smartphone, or tablet, and portable speaker (if desired for gathering music)

Group Session Guide Leader Notes

Use these notes for your own review and preparation. If desired, you can share the Main Objective, Key Scriptures, and Overview with the group at the beginning of the session in order to set the tone for the session, as well as prepare everyone for content discussion, especially those who might have been unable to complete their personal lessons during the week.

Session 1: Find One Another: Friendship Through the Lens of Biblical Community

MAIN OBJECTIVE

To understand that we are meant for connection with other believers and how we can "find one another" through true biblical friendship.

KEY SCRIPTURES

Romans 12:9-10; Romans 14:13; 2 Corinthians 13:11; 1 Thessalonians 5:11; Hebrews 10:24

OVERVIEW

This week our theme has been finding one another, which has to do with friendship through the lens of biblical community. In a world of constant connection, we find ourselves, even those of us in the body of Christ, feeling disconnected from others, though God made us for more. In the Word of God we are commanded to (among other things) be devoted to one another, honor one another, stop passing judgment on one another, encourage one another, be of one mind, build each other up, and spur one another on toward love and good deeds. We learned that God created us for community, and that in community there is risk but also great reward. We also looked at Acts 2 for insight on what community should look like and how God can unite His people despite our many differences and our selfishness. Finally, we explored our responsibilities in biblical community and how we might foster healthy and mutually beneficial community that brings praise to God.

Session 2: Fellowship with One Another: Deeper Connection Through the Lens of Biblical Community

MAIN OBJECTIVE

To see how biblical community can grow and strengthen us when we follow Jesus's lead by having a loving attitude toward others rather than a judgmental one, by living in humility, and by offering hospitality to others.

KEY SCRIPTURES

James 4:11; James 5:9; 1 Peter 4:9; 1 Peter 5:5b; 1 John 1:7

OVERVIEW

This week we learned that if we are going to thrive in biblical community, we must own up to the things we do that separate us from one another and from God. We must be willing to be vulnerable, to share both our strengths and our weaknesses, and to set aside judgments against others. When we trust God to be the Judge and focus on His righteousness, not our own, He increases our ability to see others and ourselves more clearly. Through His love, we can learn to serve others without a judgmental spirit, to live in humility, and to open our hearts and our lives to others through hospitality. In all these ways, we can make way for deeper connection with others and thrive in biblical community.

Session 3: Forgive One Another: Forgiveness Through the Lens of Biblical Community

MAIN OBJECTIVE

To understand that in order to thrive in biblical community, we must be willing to pursue peace and forgiveness and to seek restoration with God and others.

KEY SCRIPTURES:

Romans 12:16; 1 Corinthians 1:10; 2 Corinthians 13:11-12; Ephesians 4:32; Colossians 3:13; James 5:16

OVERVIEW

This week we studied about how, though we will never be able to forgive others as fully as God forgives us, we are called to live in harmony with one another; and forgiveness is a tool that can make that happen. When God calls us to forgive, He will give us the strength and the grace to do so. He will equip us as we draw on His power and love. If we convince ourselves that living in biblical community will be simple and without complications, we will be disappointed and, eventually, disillusioned. However, if we embrace the difficulties of biblical community and still choose it, we can grow in our Christlikeness. Harmony in the church is never perfect, but it can be beautiful. Even when our opinions differ (and, oh, they will), we must continually come back to the common ground of Jesus; He is enough to unite us.

Session 4: Fortify One Another: Exhortation Through the Lens of Biblical Community

MAIN OBJECTIVE

To realize that we need other believers to strengthen and encourage us, and we are called to do the same for others.

KEY SCRIPTURES

Romans 15:14; Galatians 5:13; Colossians 3:16; Hebrews 3:13; Hebrews 10:24-25; 1 Thessalonians 4:14, 18

OVERVIEW

This week we've seen that Scripture has so much to say to us about how to fortify and encourage one another. We've explored how we need the Word of God to fill us up so that we may, in turn, instruct and be instructed, encourage and be encouraged, and then give thanks to God for the process. We must spend time in God's Word and allow it to permeate who we are, how we think, and how we treat others. In order to thrive in biblical community, we must be both teachable and willing to teach, grateful and willing to give God the praise He deserves.

To fortify one another is to invest in one another's lives. As we grow in Christ, finding our tribe and learning to thrive becomes less about us and more about who God places in our lives, how we can love them better, encourage them more fully, serve them more humbly, teach them more wisely, and strengthen them more effectively.

Video Notes Answers

Week 1

Honesty

genuine

Hold on

good

Hug

affection

Honor

honor

Week 2

Learn

Lean

Lead

Week 3

Aim

Agree

Compare

fair

there

Adjust

Accept

Week 4

Full

goodness

Filled

knowledge

Fit

instruct

Notes

Introduction

1. David Rosenfelt, *Dogtripping: 25 Rescues, 11 Volunteers, and 3 RVs on Our Canine Cross-Country Adventure.* Kindle edition, Chapter 1, "Dread and More Dread."
2. Bible Tools, s.v., "allelon," https://www.bibletools.org/index.cfm/fuseaction/Lexicon.show/ID/G240/allelon.htm. Accessed February 12, 2020.

Week 1

1. Glenn Hohnberg, "Isolation Destroys Us," The Gospel Coalition (Australia Edition), December 27, 2018, https://au.thegospelcoalition.org/article/isolation-destroys-us/. Accessed February 14, 2020.
2. "Romans 14—Helping a Weaker Brother," Enduring Word, https://enduringword.com/bible-commentary/romans-14/. Accessed February 14, 2020.
3. Ashley Wooldridge (@ashleywooldrige), "Met an amazing group of people at our CCV East Valley campus today," Instagram photo, July 7, 2019, https://www.instagram.com/p/BzoW53GHP8S/.
4. Lloyd John Ogilvie, *Drumbeat of Love* (Waco, TX: Word, 1976), 197.
5. "What's to Know about Alopecia Areata?" Medical News Today, https://www.medicalnewstoday.com/articles/70956.php. Accessed February 14, 2020.

Week 2

1. Rick Warren, *The Purpose Driven Life: What on Earth Am I Here For?* (Grand Rapids, MI: Zondervan, 2002),148.
2. Merriam-Webster, s.v. "koinonia," https://www.merriam-webster.com/dictionary/koinonia. Accessed February 17, 2020.
3. "Hospital—Origin of the Word," Christian Forums, https://www.christianforums.com/threads/hospital-origin-of-the-word.7702385/. Accessed February 17, 2020.
4. Henry T. Blackaby and Melvin D. Blackaby, *Experiencing God Together: God's Plan to Touch Your World* (Nashville: B & H Publishing Group, 2002), 34–35.

Week 3

1. Louie Giglio, "Man in the Mirror: Part 1," https://www.life.church/media/man-in-the-mirror/man-in-the-mirror/. Accessed February 18, 2020.
2. "Forgiveness: Your Health Depends on It," https://www.hopkinsmedicine.org/health/wellness-and-prevention/forgiveness-your-health-depends-on-it. Accessed February 18, 2020.
3. "Verse-by-Verse Bible Commentary: 1 Corinthians 1:10," https://www.studylight.org/commentary/1-corinthians/1-10.html. Accessed February 18, 2020.

Week 4

1. Kirk Johnson, "Who Is Really Making 'Chihuly Art'?" *New York Times*, August 21, 2017, https://www.nytimes.com/2017/08/21/arts/design/chihuly-glass-bipolar-court-moi.html.
2. "How the Crabs in a Bucket Mentality Is Holding You Back," *Develop Good Habits*, December 18, 2019, https://www.developgoodhabits.com/crabs-bucket/. Accessed February 18, 2020.
3. Simon Spacey, "Crab Mentality, Cyberbullying and 'Name and Shame' Rankings," April 19, 2015, https://pdfs.semanticscholar.org/3e43/a0f74b4111c41513f2e0d0a13c92e79efb18.pdf. Accessed February 19, 2020.
4. Vocabulary.com, s.v. "encourage," https://www.vocabulary.com/dictionary/encourage. Accessed February 19, 2020.

Made in the USA
Middletown, DE
19 September 2024

61133958R00091